4-21-75

Cash Management

Cash Management

An Inventory Control
Limit Approach

Richard Homonoff
Boston Economic Associates, Inc.

David Wiley Mullins, Jr.
Harvard University

Lexington Books
D.C. Heath and Company
Lexington, Massachusetts
Toronto   London

Library of Congress Cataloging in Publication Data

Homonoff, Richard B.
  Cash management.

  Bibliography: p.
  Includes index.
  1. Corporations—Cash position. 2. Inventory control. 3. Corporations—Finance. I. Mullins, David Wiley, joint author. II. Title.
  HG4028.C45H64   658.1'5   74-23318
  ISBN 0-669-97485-4

Copyright © 1975 by D.C. Heath and Company.

All rights reserved. No part of this publication may be reproduced or transmitted in any form or by any means, electronic or mechanical, including photocopy, recording, or any information storage or retrieval system, without permission in writing from the publisher.

Published simultaneously in Canada.

Printed in the United States of America.

International Standard Book Number: 0-669-97485-4

Library of Congress Catalog Card Number: 74-23318

Contents

	List of Figures	ix
	List of Tables	xi
	Preface	xiii
	Acknowledgments	xv
Chapter 1	Introduction	3
	1-1 Background	3
	1-2 The Problem	4
Chapter 2	The Basic Miller-Orr Model	7
Chapter 3	Firm A: Traditional Cash Management	11
Chapter 4	Statistical Analysis of Firm A's Cash Flow Data	15
	Appendix 4A	25
Chapter 5	Decision Models with an Absolute Minimum Cash Balance Constraint	33
	5-1 Introduction	33
	5-2 The Miller-Orr Two-asset Model	33
	5-3 Orr's Three-asset Model	36
	5-4 The Need for Extension of the Miller-Orr Model	37
	5-5 Simulation as a Test of the Models	38
	5-6 Examples of the Application of the Simulation Model	40

	5-7 The Two-asset Asymmetric Transaction Cost Model	43
	5-8 The "Matched Loading" Model	45
	5-9 The Four- and Five-asset Symmetric Transaction Cost Model	50
	5-10 Questions on the Appropriateness of the Absolute Minimum Cash Balance Constraint	53
	Appendix 5A: Some Characteristics of the Two-asset Cost Function	55
	Appendix 5B: The Sensitivity of the Two-asset Miller-Orr Minimum Cost, $E(C)$, to Changes in Exogenous Variables	59
Chapter 6	**Decision Models with a Minimum Average Cash Balance Constraint**	61
	6-1 Introduction	61
	6-2 Approaches to the Minimum Average Cash Balance Constraint	61
	6-3 The "Relaxed" Minimum Average Cash Balance Model with Penalties	62
	6-4 Adjusting Miller-Orr Type Models to the Minimum Average Cash Balance Constraint	69
	6-5 Observations on the Minimum Average Cash Constraint Models	73
	Appendix 6A: Derivations of the "Relaxed" Minimum Average Cash Balance Model with Penalties	75
Chapter 7	**A Simulation Approach to Cash Management**	79
Chapter 8	**Forecasting in Cash Management**	89
Chapter 9	**Conclusion**	93

Bibliography 97

Index 101

About the Authors 105

List of Figures

2-1	The Basic Miller-Orr Model	9
4-1	Frequency Distribution of Firm A's Daily Cash Flows for 11-Month Period	18
4-2	Frequency Distribution of Firm A's Daily Cash Flows by Month	19
4-3	Average Daily Cash Flows by Day of the Month	22
5A-1	The Probability Density Functions $f_{\widetilde{M}}(M)$ and $f_{\widetilde{w}}(w)$	58
6-1	The Penalty/Opportunity Cost Loss Function	65
6-2	Approximation of the Penalty/Opportunity Cost Loss Function	66

List of Tables

3-1	Characteristics of Firm A's Cash Flows and Cash Management Policy	12
3-2	Firm A's Interest Revenue from Earning Assets	14
4-1	Daily Means and Standard Deviations of Daily Cash Flows by Month	17
4-2	Analysis of Variance Results	20
4-3	Coefficients of Treatments and Blocks from Analysis of Variance	23
5-1	An 11-Month Three-asset Simulation Using Firm A's Implicit Costs per Transaction	40
5-2	Two-asset Symmetric Transaction Cost Miller-Orr Model with Absolute Minimum Cash Constraint	42
5-3	Results of the Iterative Computation of b_0 for Use in the Two-asset Asymmetric Transaction Cost Model	45
5-4	Two-asset Asymmetric Transaction Cost Miller-Orr Model with Absolute Minimum Cash Constraint	46
5-5	Solutions to the Matched Loading Control Limits for Different Costs per Transaction (b) and Different Planning Period Lengths (N)	48
5-6	Matched Loading Model with Absolute Minimum Cash Constraint	49
5-7	Status Definitions for the Four- and Five-asset Models	50

6-1	Two-asset Symmetric Transaction Cost Model with Penalty Function on "Relaxed" Average Cash Constraint	68
6-2	"Adjusted" Two-asset Symmetric Transaction Cost Miller-Orr Model with Minimum Average Cash Constraint	70
6-3	"Adjusted" Two-asset Asymmetric Transaction Cost Miller-Orr Model with Minimum Average Cash Constraint	71
6-4	"Adjusted" Matched Loading Model with Minimum Average Cash Constraint	72
7-1 to 7-7	Summary of Average Daily Profits after Penalty Cost under Different Policies— with the Following Models:	
7-1	Symmetric Miller-Orr Model with Absolute Minimum Constraint	81
7-2	Asymmetric Miller-Orr Model with Absolute Minimum Constraint	82
7-3	Matched Load Miller-Orr Model with Absolute Minimum Constraint	83
7-4	Symmetric Model with Penalty and Relaxed Average Constraint	84
7-5	Symmetric Miller-Orr Model with Minimum Average Constraint	85
7-6	Asymmetric Miller-Orr Model with Minimum Average Constraint	86
7-7	Matched Load Miller-Orr Model with Minimum Average Constraint	87
8-1	Firm A's Implicit Forecasts	92

Preface

This book addresses the problem of corporate cash management. The models and approaches developed for minimizing the cost of managing short-term funds will be of interest to professional managers and academic researchers alike.

The application of inventory control theory to cash management was first used by monetary theorists to explain certain macroeconomic phenomena. In this book these early approaches are modified to meet the pragmatic requirements of corporate financial managers.

The focus of this book is the development of "naive" cash management models. Naive models are based on simple, but reasonable, assumptions; the only assumptions and constraints incorporated in the models of this book are those necessary to meet the realities of decisionmaking in a managerial environment. The naive models have several advantages over both the "seat-of-the-pants" approach and the very complex operations research models for managing cash. First, the naive models develop very simple decision rules for day-to-day management. These rules are both intuitively satisfying to managers and easy to execute by clerical personnel. Both the seat-of-the-pants approach and the complex model approach make significant demands on managerial time either for the actual decisions or for the collection and incorporation of forecast data and the execution of the more complex decision procedures. The second advantage of naive models is that the day-to-day operating procedure is systematic and routinized, yet it minimizes costs while meeting external banking constraints. Third, the models can be used to develop managers' insight into the cash management process.

One issue that arises in the discussion of cash management is the importance and utility of forecast information. A comparison of a naive model with a model that actively utilizes forecasts of cash flows is presented. There follows an analysis of the circumstances under which the naive model outperforms the more complex model.

The efficacy of these naive models is demonstrated through a case study from the business world.

Acknowledgments

We owe an enormous intellectual debt to Professors Merton Miller and Daniel Orr for their pioneering and insightful research. The extent of the debt will be obvious to the readers of this book.

This book is the result of research performed by the authors at the Massachusetts Institute of Technology, Sloan School of Management. A number of people have contributed guidance and assistance to its development, and we wish to express publicly our indebtedness to those most actively involved.

Professor Myron Scholes introduced us to the Miller-Orr model and the application of inventory control theory to cash management. He has offered creative suggestions and critical analysis of our work and has helped us understand the implications of our findings.

Professor Warren Hausman has given us consultation on inventory control models and assistance with some of the mathematical analysis. He, too, has offered constructive criticism and, along with Professor Robert Merton, has suggested some dynamic programing approaches to the cash management problem.

Professor Glen Urban contributed advice and criticism concerning the statistical analysis and exploratory data analysis in the early stages of the development of this book.

We owe a tremendous debt to the assistant treasurer and staff of Firm A. They provided us with the data necessary to parameterize our models and evaluate our simulations. Furthermore, they spent a considerable amount of time giving us the benefit of their insight into the cash management problem and the utility of our models. The assistant treasurer has asked that the corporation remain unnamed.

Janice Smaga made significant contributions to the exploratory data analysis phase of this project and later to the statistical analysis. She also typed the manuscript, and we are most grateful for her good humor and help.

Emeline Homonoff also lent clerical and emotional support to this work. Her assistance in the writing stage is greatly appreciated. We also wish to thank Patti Scott for her fine job of copyediting the manuscript.

All electronic computations were performed at the Information Processing Center of M.I.T.

We thank the President and Fellows of Harvard College for permitting us to adapt a figure from the Miller-Orr article: "A Model of the Demand for Money by Firms" (*Quarterly Journal of Economics*, Vol. 53, August 1966, p. 420.)

Finally, each author claims sole credit for whatever is creative and useful in this book and blames the other for errors and omissions!

Cash Management

1 Introduction

1-1 Background

J.M. Keynes stated that there are three motives for holding money (i.e., for liquidity preference): the transactions motive, the precautionary motive, and the speculative motive. The transactions motive relates to "holding cash to bridge the interval between the receipt of income and its disbursement [or] between the time of incurring business costs and that of the receipt of the sale-proceeds." The precautionary motive concerns holding cash to provide "for contingencies requiring sudden expenditure and for unforeseen opportunities of advantage purchases." The speculative motive involves holding cash in order to secure "profit from knowing better than the market what the future will bring forth"; in other words, this motive is a function of expectations. Keynes believed the transactions motive and the precautionary motive to be essentially functions of the level of income (i.e., the money value of the transactions) and the speculative motive to be a function of interest rate.[a] In this book, we concern ourselves with the transactions demand for cash, in particular the management of corporate cash balances.

W.J. Baumol investigated a rational firm's transactions demand for cash by formulating its transactions demand decisions as a deterministic inventory control problem.[b] He assumed a firm with a constant, continuous drain of cash reserves which periodically converted some of its assets to cash to ensure a positive cash balance. He formulated two costs: the opportunity cost of keeping cash assets greater than zero (a function of the interest rate), and the "brokerage" cost of converting assets to cash. The second cost had been ignored by theorists prior to Baumol. He then computed the cash demand for a rational firm that tried to minimize costs. Unlike Keynes, who believed that the transactions demand for cash was a function of only the income of the firm, Baumol found that the transactions demand was a function of both income and interest rate.

M.H. Miller and D. Orr brought more sophistication to Baumol's formulation and expanded his findings.[c] They assumed that the series of positive and

---

[a]John M. Keynes. *The General Theory of Employment, Interest and Money.* 1936. Chapters 13 and 15. New York: Harcourt Brace Jovanovich, Inc.
[b]William J. Baumol. "The Transactions Demand for Cash: An Inventory Theoretic Approach." *Quarterly Journal of Economics*, 11, 1952, pp. 545-556.
[c]Merton H. Miller and Daniel Orr. "A Model of the Demand for Money by Firms." *Quarterly Journal of Economics*, 80, 1966, pp. 413-435.

negative cash inflows to a firm were generated by a Gaussian function $N(0,\sigma^2)$. They assumed that there were only two assets of interest: cash and interest-bearing securities. The decision rules for conversion between cash and securities are based on thresholds which are set so as to minimize Baumol's cost function (see Chapter 2). Miller and Orr found that the resultant demand for cash was a function of both the interest rate and the variance of the cash flows. Variance is a function of both income level and the synchronization, or coordination, between inflows and outflows in the firm. Hence, the transactions demand for cash is responsive to income, interest rate, and synchronization.

1-2 The Problem

The transactions cash management problem typically belongs to a high-level financial officer of a firm (i.e., assistant treasurer or assistant controller). That role is basically reactive, for the financial officer has little control over inflows and outflows of the firm's cash resulting from transactions. Costless opportunities to control flows are limited. Other methods of affecting flows are implemented at a cost and are part of the reactive control policy. Such methods do not change the basic generation of cash flows. Lack of control and inability to forecast cash flows are especially characteristic of central cash balances of larger corporations. As their cash needs fluctuate, the firm's divisions feed and draw upon such balances.

A firm is not able to earn interest on its idle cash balances kept in commercial banks. Therefore it has an incentive to invest excess cash in interest-earning securities such as commercial paper (CP), treasury bills (TB), certificates of deposit (CD), repurchase agreements (RP), or other money-market instruments. Such securities differ in interest return, risk, maturity, and marketability. The financial officer invests in such securities in an attempt to economize on idle cash balances, but the investment is limited by the costs of transferring funds into and out of securities to meet transactions demands. The opportunity cost of idle balances and transfer costs constitute the Baumol and Miller-Orr cost functions. However, the financial officer is bound by other constraints, both external and self-imposed. For example, in return for services provided to a firm, banks require the maintenance of an absolute minimum or a minimum average cash balance in demand deposits. This balance is called the "compensating balance" and is in lieu of a service charge. An example of a self-imposed constraint is a policy of not selling negotiable CDs before maturity, to avoid large transaction costs and inconvenience to the issuing bank. Another example might be an a priori elimination of certain securities from consideration (for example, CPs because of the default risk). Often policy rules of thumb are developed which define the types and proportions of securities eligible for the short-term portfolio.

We now restate the financial officer's problem: Maximize expected interest revenue minus expected transaction cost, subject to (1) compensating balance constraints, and (2) policy constraints. An additional point to note is that transaction costs include not only "visible" costs such as wiring charges, telephone bills, brokerage and portfolio management fees, but also "invisible" costs such as overhead, accounting, and management time. Although neglect of invisible costs may lead to a misallocation of corporate resources, reward systems tend to ignore such costs.

There is room for disagreement with the Baumol-Miller-Orr objective function as just formulated. Some argue that the opportunity cost of idle balance is the cost of capital of the firm—a value considerably higher than the return of short-term securities. Cash is viewed as a scarce and costly productive resource. High-return projects await funding, and compensating balances cover not only a payment for bank services but also ordinary transaction activity. In such a case, the objective is to maintain cash balances at the absolute minimum required by banks. A very aggressive control policy is undertaken in pursuit of this goal. Although in our book we do not consider this "sharp pencil" approach in detail, we do touch upon it in Chapter 8.

This book deals with the modeling of the cash management process of an unnamed firm (Firm A). The basic Miller-Orr model is outlined in Chapter 2 and Firm A is described in Chapters 3 and 4. In Chapters 5 and 6 we apply the Miller-Orr model to Firm A's problem and derive analytical extensions of the model appropriate to Firm A's environment. In Chapter 7 a flexible simulation approach to cash management is developed, and in Chapter 8 we consider some observations of Firm A's current approach as well as an alternative approach to cash management. Finally, in Chapter 9 our work is briefly summarized and future research opportunities are delineated.

The objective of this book is the development of flexible, realistic approaches to cash management which managers can easily understand, implement, and use, and which significantly increase the effectiveness of their decisionmaking.

2 The Basic Miller-Orr Model

The Miller-Orr model incorporates several basic assumptions concerning the nature of a firm's cash management problem.

First, it assumes only two assets: the firm's cash balances, and a portfolio of earning assets which yield i dollars per dollar per day. The earning assets are assumed to be relatively short-term money-market instruments such as certificates of deposit (CD) or treasury bills (TB).

Transfers between the two assets take place at a marginal cost of b dollars per transfer regardless of the size or direction of transfer. Transfers may take place at any time and are assumed to be instantaneous.

The firm is assumed to have an exogenous constraint on its cash balance in the form of a compensating-balance requirement. This requirement is, in effect, a payment for banking services and serves to set the absolute level of the Miller-Orr control policy. While the requirement can take one of two forms, the Miller-Orr model is derived for a constraint which prohibits cash balances from falling below some specified amount. Specifically, the model requires that the firm's cash balance never be allowed to fall below zero. The second form, which requires the maintenance of some average cash balance over a specific time period, is the basis of models described in Chapter 6.

The cash flows are assumed to be stochastic—generating a stationary random walk in cash balances. In the simplest form, the distribution of cash flows has a zero mean. Cash inflows and outflows behave as a sequence of independent Bernoulli trials, such that in a small fraction of the working day, $1/t$ (that is, an hour), cash balances will increase by $+m$ with a probability $p = 1/2$ and will decrease by $-m$ with a probability $q = (1-p) = 1/2$. Hence, over a number of days, n, the distribution of changes in the cash balance is binomial with mean $\mu = ntm(p-q) = 0$ and variance $\sigma^2 = ntm^2$. As n increases, this binomial distribution approaches a normal distribution.

The firm's objective is to minimize the steady-state cost of managing the cash balance under a naive control policy. The naive policy employed is a two-parameter control limit model. Such a policy allows the cash balance to fluctuate freely until the upper or lower limit (h and 0 respectively) is violated. The decision rule calls for a transfer of $h - z$ dollars into earning assets when the cash balance reaches h, and a transfer of z dollars out of earning assets when the cash balance wanders to zero. The aim of the policy is to minimize the expected cost per day of managing the cash balance with respect to the upper limit h and the return point z. This expected daily cost, $E(C)$, comprises two parts: the expected transactions cost (probability of transfer multiplied by the cost per transfer b), and the expected opportunity cost of holding cash (the expected cash balanced multiplied by i, the earning rate on securities).

The solution for optimal h and z involves first finding the steady-state occupancy probability distribution of cash balances, and then carrying out the following minimization:

$$\min_{h,z} E(C) = \frac{b \sigma^2}{z(h-z)} + \frac{i(h+z)}{3}$$

where σ^2 is the daily variance of changes in the cash balance ($m^2 t$). The solution yields

$$z_{opt} = \left(\frac{3 b \sigma^2}{4 i} \right)^{1/3}$$

$$h_{opt} = 3 z_{opt}$$

$$\overline{M} = \text{average cash balance} = (4/3) z_{opt}$$

The solution yields the curious result that despite the symmetry of cash flows and transfer costs, the return point is not $(1/2)h$ as one might suspect; rather it is $(1/3)h$ regardless of the values of i and b. The result follows from the nature of the cost function.

The assumptions underlying the basic Miller-Orr model (see Figure 2-1) have been the subject of much investigation. Such study includes sensitivity analyses and analytical extensions concerning both the nature of the cash flows (i.e., drift, asymmetry of cash flows, Paretian rather than Gaussian flows, pooling of separate distributions, irregularly timed transactions, and so on) and the objective function (i.e., proportional transfer costs, combinations of lumpy and proportional costs, and so forth). The question of the optimality of the policy form has been investigated, and the model has been extended to three assets. These refinements, as well as discussions of the model's implications for aggregative analysis, are reviewed in detail by Orr (1970) and therefore will not be delineated here. However, one important implication of much of this work should be noted. The basic Miller-Orr model seems to fare surprisingly well despite relatively wide violations of its simple underlying assumptions. This robustness strongly suggests its utility not only as an abstract economic model but also as an applied managerial tool.

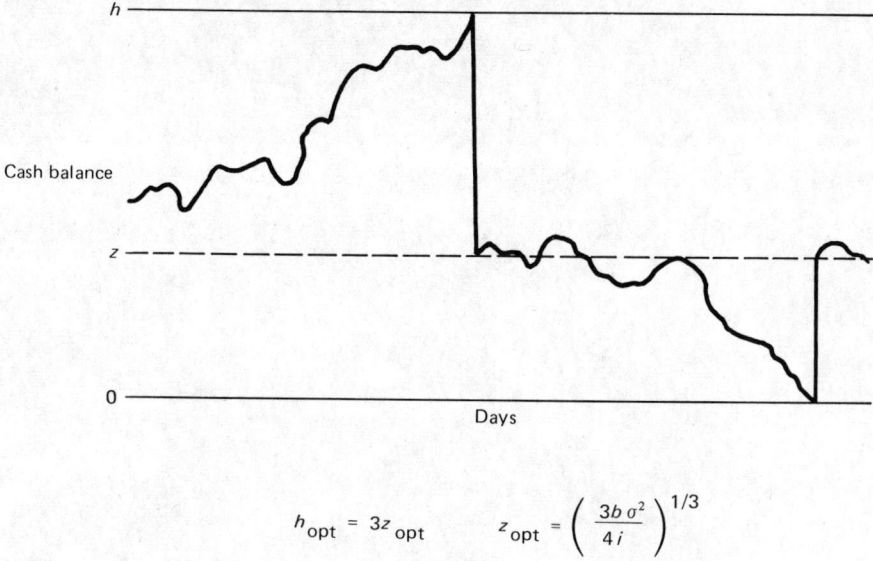

Figure 2-1. The Basic Miller-Orr Model. Source: Adapted with permission of the copyright holders from Merton H. Miller and D. Orr, "A Model of the Demand for Money by Firms," *Quarterly Journal of Economics*, Vol. 53, August 1966, p. 420.

3 Firm A: Traditional Cash Management

In 1971 Firm A had sales of $180 million generated by eleven divisions throughout the United States. Government sales account for approximately one-half of this volume. Cash management is the job of the assistant treasurer and staff. The assistant treasurer and two subordinates are involved in this daily task. They provided us with extensive data including daily cash flows from February 1971 through December 1971. Our discussion compares their approach to cash management with the assumptions underlying the Miller-Orr model outlined in Chapter 2.

First, unlike the Miller-Orr assumption of only two assets, Firm A's policy involves three assets—cash, repurchase agreements (RPs), and certificates of deposit (CDs). Excess cash is invested either in RPs ("overnights") with a maturity of 1 day or in 120-day CDs. Various characteristics of their cash management approach are summarized in Table 3-1. The use of three assets can be handled in extended versions of the Miller-Orr model.

The assumption that transactions can take place at any time and are virtually instantaneous was supported by the managers. They also agreed with the assumption of a fixed (versus proportional) transfer cost regardless of size or direction of transfer. However, they considered this cost negligible, since the employee's time is often used in communicating with money markets and since there are no portfolio management fees. They admitted fixed charges for wiring and occasionally for telephone charges but felt that a fixed charge of greater than $2 per transfer would be unrealistic. The authors disagree with this evaluation of transfer cost. We feel this charge is perhaps much higher, for management time spent on transfers is a marginal cost if productive use of such time in alternative activities can be assumed, and the accounting overhead generated by such transfers may be significant. We feel that omission of such "invisible" costs may be the result of reward systems which tend to ignore such costs, while the offsetting revenue (i.e., interest return) is highly visible. A more realistic estimate of b (the cost of transfer) might be in the range of $10 to $20. A final point must be made about transfer costs. Firm A recognized the high, proportional transaction charge involved in selling CDs before maturity. However, Firm A has a policy of never selling CDs before maturity. Hence, they consider the transfer costs of buying securities and of maturing securities roughly fixed and equal. Thus, the often criticized assumption of the Miller-Orr model concerning lumpy transfer costs is supported in this case.

Firm A's compensating-balance constraint is in the form of a minimum

Table 3-1
Characteristics of Firm A's Cash Flows and Cash Management Policy[a]

Period		Total	Feb.	Mar.	Apr.	May	June	July	Aug.	Sept.	Oct.	Nov.	Dec.
Number of business days		231	19	23	22	20	22	21	22	21	21	17	23
Net Cash Flows	Daily Mean	4	−73	36	98	5	−11	131	9	−105	−65	−40	35
	Daily Standard Deviation	581	500	493	635	533	575	834	383	760	488	669	506
Cash Balance	Daily Mean	3,568	4,003	4,362	3,735	4,018	3,881	3,695	2,935	2,861	2,946	3,523	3,297
	Daily Standard Deviation	839	1,402	722	816	512	268	447	447	650	437	873	587
RP Balance	Daily Mean	925	26	196	1,206	990	1,025	1,690	1,497	592	369	179	2,090
	Daily Standard Deviation	970	114	517	868	845	893	1,100	522	696	646	118	866
CD Balance	Daily Mean	3,687	2,283	1,928	2,195	3,220	3,166	4,500	6,686	6,150	4,693	3,903	1,999
	Daily Standard Deviation	1,696	819	333	924	511	402	787	283	251	451	539	265
RP + CD Balance	Daily Mean	4,612	2,309	2,123	3,401	4,210	4,191	6,190	8,183	6,742	5,062	4,082	4,089
	Daily Standard Deviation	1,978	834	621	1,219	782	1,069	1,315	465	858	798	447	860
Total Balance	Daily Mean	8,179	6,311	6,486	7,136	8,228	8,072	9,886	11,117	9,603	8,008	7,605	7,386
	Daily Standard Deviation	1,681	696	945	1,195	801	936	1,003	597	935	1,036	857	739

[a] All daily means and daily standard deviations are expressed in $000.

average balance and, therefore, is not consistent with the Miller-Orr assumption of an absolute minimum balance. Corporate headquarters of Firm A has accounts with four major big-city banks in three large metropolitan areas. In return for money-market services, a $10 million line of credit, and other services, Firm A was required to maintain average demand deposits of approximately $3 million during 1971. There is a fairly high degree of fluctuation around this compensating balance in Firm A's data (see Table 3-1).

The statistical assumptions concerning the nature of cash flows are considered in more detail in Chapter 4. However, a few preliminary points are worth noting here. The cash balance considered here is Firm A's central cash balance at corporate headquarters. The divisions have separate accounts for their local transactions, and they feed and draw upon the corporate balances to meet their needs. Although divisions forecast their cash flows, the assistant treasurer believes that these forecasts are highly inaccurate and of little use in managing the corporate cash balance. Inflows from the government's half of Firm A's business are particularly unpredictable. Thus, the managers recognize significant unpredictable elements in their cash flows, and this is reflected in their policies. However, their cash management policies also depend on their contention that they can predict certain elements in cash flows. Such elements include a large monthly payment to one supplier, tax and payroll outflows, and certain predictable inflows. In later chapters we will test these contentions and examine whether cash management based upon naive assumptions of random flows in the Miller-Orr model performs as well as the current approach based partly on predictable flows.

Firm A has developed policy rules to guide its cash management. First, the only earning assets considered are CDs and RPs, although in the past some CPs were bought. CDs are never sold before maturity because of the high transaction cost incurred and because of inconvenience to the issuing banks. The inflexibility imposed by this policy is offset by investment in the other earning asset, RPs bearing a lower interest rate and a maturity of 1 day. The stated policy is to maintain a $1 million investment in RPs (requiring two transfers per day) as a buffer between cash and CDs, although the data show considerable fluctuation around this value (see Table 3-1). According to the assistant treasurer, the $1 million figure was selected because they expect an outflow of that magnitude about once a month. A $1 million daily outflow occurs in the data about once every month and a half. The choice of such a large figure for the RP target balance manifests their commitment to the policy of not discounting CDs, their belief that RP transfer costs are negligible, and their recognition of significant stochastic elements in cash flows.

Given their constraints, Firm A's cash management policy is to use their staff's knowledge and experience concerning predictable cash flows, float times, etc., to maximize interest revenue (see Table 3-2) subject to meeting transactions demand. The assistant treasurer's staff selects CD maturity dates and makes daily portfolio decisions in pursuit of their objective. As we mentioned earlier, transfer costs are not considered a significant element in their approach to this problem.

Table 3-2
Firm A's Interest Revenue from Earning Assets

Period	Revenue in $
January	10,200
February	10,800
March	7,000
April	11,600
May	16,800
June	16,900
July	28,100
August	38,500
September	32,200
October	25,700
November	20,000
December	17,500
Total	235,300

4 Statistical Analysis of Firm A's Cash Flow Data

The Miller-Orr model rests on the assumption that cash inflows and outflows are stochastic, generated by a Gaussian function. Orr (1970) reports sensitivity analyses of the cash flow assumptions, including investigations of nonstationary cash flows, the symmetry assumption of the Bernoulli process, excessive concentration of cash flows in the tails of the distribution, and other factors. In this chapter we examine Firm A's cash flows. The assumption of normality is analyzed, and a test of serial correlation is reported. The stationarity of the distribution of cash flows is discussed, and we test for the existence of systematic elements in the cash flows.

A Kolmogorov-Smirnov test for normality (Appendix 4A, Section 4A-1) on the 231 days of data failed to reject the hypothesis that the distribution is normal at a level of significance[a] $\alpha = 0.01$. However, we can reject the hypothesis that the flows are normally distributed at a level of significance $\alpha = 0.05$. The test shows that the distribution deviates from the normal distribution in sections near the center of the distribution. This failure may be caused by extreme outliers which enlarge the variance of the theoretical distribution and thus decrease the expected proportion of events in the midsections of the distribution. This phenomenon has been observed in other studies (Miller-Orr, 1968; Orr, 1970). One hypothesis is that the flows are Paretian rather than Gaussian, which contradicts the analytical assumptions underlying the model. If the daily cash flows are truly Paretian, the development of a different, and possibly more complex, cash management model would be necessary. However, a more intuitive explanation for the statistical findings might be that such behavior is the result of the pooling or mixing of two distinct Bernoulli processes. Paretian symptoms can result from the mixing of two Gaussian populations with the same mean, one population having a larger variance and a smaller probability of occurring in the mix. Such an explanation is attractive. It seems reasonable that the distribution of certain large cash flows (e.g., payroll, taxes, dividends, etc.) is radically different from the distribution of normal daily cash flows. Therefore, one would expect large tails in the distribution of cash flows.

---

[a]The classical testing procedure considers the problem of whether to reject a null hypothesis. The test generates a value which has a certain probability of occurring under the null hypothesis. If the probability of an observed test value is less than some "cutoff" probability, the null hypothesis is rejected. This cutoff probability is designated by the character α and is called the "level of significance."

In examining this possibility, we retested for normality, deleting from the distribution those outliers beyond the 3σ level (6 outliers). We also tested after deleting 12 outliers—those beyond the 2σ level in the original distribution. Table 4-1 displays the monthly means and standard deviations of the cash flows with no outliers removed, with 6 outliers removed, and with 12 outliers removed. The Kolmogorov-Smirnov tests on data with 6 and 12 outliers removed (Appendix 4A, Sections 4A-2 and 4A-3) show that one cannot reject the hypothesis that the resulting distributions are normal at a level of significance $\alpha = 0.10$. This evidence suggests that one might consider the bulk of daily cash flows as normally distributed and the majority of outliers as generated by a different distribution. The pooling of separate Bernoulli processes does not result in serious errors in the model's prediction of mean cash balances and passage times (Orr, 1970). However, there is no reason to believe that the large flow distribution should be normal. We might reasonably assume some other distribution (Poisson, for instance) which might result in poor performance by the model. The performance of the model in this case is discussed in later chapters.

Another assumption of the model is the independence of daily cash flows. A runs test on the data rejects the hypothesis that the ordering is not random, with a significance level $\alpha = 0.05$ (Appendix 4A, Section 4A-4). Here again, the precise assumptions are violated. The important question is how this violation affects the performance of the model.

Another requirement of the Miller-Orr approach is stability of the parameters of the cash flow distribution. If the mean and variance of cash flows fluctuate significantly from month to month, the model will not perform well. Predictable fluctuations such as seasonal factors might be incorporated in the cash management process by adjusting the parameters of the model. The existence of a stable nonzero mean would require the use of a more complex version of the model. However, there is no method for dealing with unpredictable fluctuations in the mean and variance of cash flows.

Firm A's sales are concentrated in rapidly changing technological fields. This fact, plus the general perturbations in the economy during 1971, gives no a priori reason to expect the required stability in cash flows. Nonetheless, Firm A's cash flow exhibits such stability. The frequency distribution of net cash inflows for the full period is shown in Figure 4-1. The distribution has a mean of $4,000 and a standard deviation of approximately $580,000. These figures indicate the zero-drift case. Clearly, the mean is not significantly different from zero. Thus we are assured that the complex, nonzero-mean "drift" model will not be needed in this case. Confidence limits on the mean and variance of the full distribution are reported in Appendix 4A, Section 4A-5.

The distributions of the daily cash flows by month are shown in Figure 4-2. None of the monthly means were significantly different from zero or from the overall mean, even at a level of significance $\alpha = 0.30$. This fact illustrates the remarkable stability of the process throughout the year and the lack of

Table 4-1
Daily Means and Standard Deviations of Daily Cash Flows by Month[a]

Period		Total	Feb.	Mar.	Apr.	May	June	July	Aug.	Sept.	Oct.	Nov.	Dec.
With no Outliers Removed	Days	231	19	23	22	20	22	21	22	21	21	17	23
	Daily Mean	4	−73	36	98	5	−11	131	9	−105	−65	−40	35
	Daily Standard Deviation	581	500	493	635	533	575	834	383	760	488	669	506
With 6 Outliers Removed	Days	225	19	23	21	20	21	20	22	19	21	16	23
	Daily Mean	3	−73	36	−3	5	82	16	9	−92	−65	82	35
	Daily Standard Deviation	467	500	493	437	533	387	666	383	261	488	453	506
With 12 Outliers Removed	Days	219	19	23	21	18	21	18	22	19	20	15	23
	Daily Mean	1	−73	36	−3	−14	82	−4	9	−92	12	−7	35
	Daily Standard Deviation	407	500	493	437	302	387	487	383	261	346	288	506

[a] All daily means and daily standard deviations are expressed in $000.

```
                        -2,600  X
                        -2,400
                        -2,200
                        -2,000  XX
                        -1,800
                        -1,600  X
                        -1,400  XX
                        -1,200  X
                        -1,000  XXXXXX
   Daily Net Cash Flows (C) in $000
                        - 800   XXX
                        - 600   XXXXXXXXXXXXXXXXXXXXXXX
                        - 400   XXXXXXXXXXXXXXXXXXXXXXXXXXXXXX
                        - 200   XXXXXXXXXXXXXXXXXXXXXXXXXXXXXXXXXXXXXXXXXX
                        -   0   XXXXXXXXXXXXXXXXXXXXXXXXXXXXXXXXXXXXXXXXXXXXXXX
                          200   XXXXXXXXXXXXXXXXXXXXXXXXXXXXX
                          400   XXXXXXXXXXXXX
                          600   XXXXXXXXX
                          800   XXXXX
                        1,000   XXXX
                        1,200
                        1,400   XX
                        1,600   X
                        1,800                                   C̄  = 4.0
                        2,000   X                               S_c = 581
                        2,200   X
                        2,400   X
                        2,600   X
```

Figure 4-1. Frequency Distribution of Firm A's Daily Cash Flows for 11-Month Period.

systematic seasonal effects as well. Such stability augurs well for the use of the Miller-Orr approach.

As one might expect from the previous discussion of an excessive number of large flows in the distribution, the monthly variances, although relatively stable, do not exhibit the stability reflected in monthly means. A 99% confidence interval, centered on the variance of the overall period and the average monthly sample size ($N = 21$), is violated by the low variance in August. The August variance is significantly different from the overall variance (excluding August) at the 99% level of confidence (see Appendix 4A, Section 4A-6, for the F tests and additional details). The largest variance, that of July, is also significantly different from the overall variance (excluding July) at the 99% level of confidence. These differences may be the result of some perturbation related to summer vacation scheduling. All the other monthly variances are not significantly different from the overall variance at the 99% level. Therefore, the variance is relatively stable over the period. Evaluation of the performance of the model will indicate the severity of the instability in variances.

The fact that the distribution is normal without seasonal effects does not ensure the absence of systematic, predictable daily or weekly effects. If present,

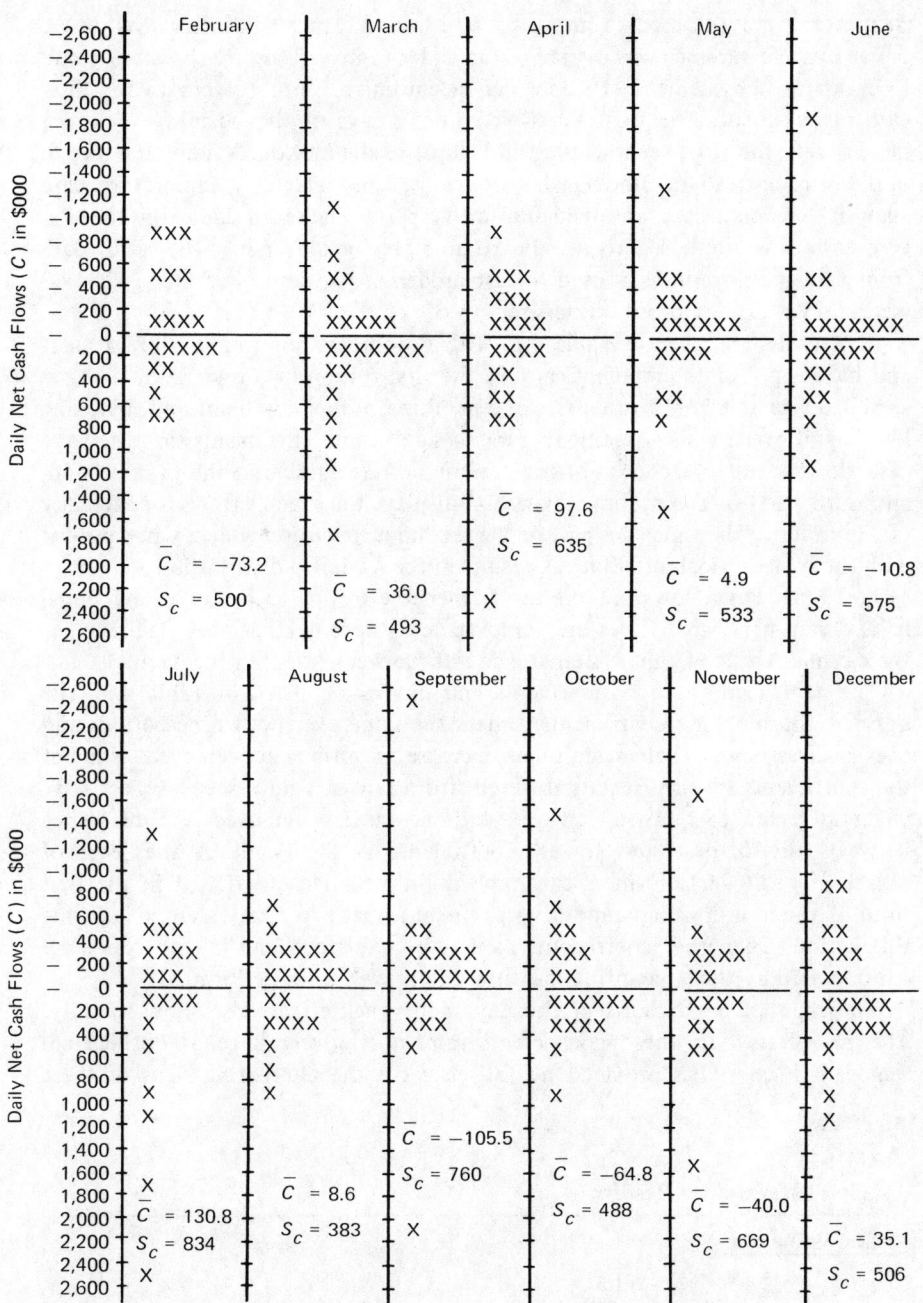

Figure 4-2. Frequency Distribution of Firm A's Daily Cash Flows by Month.

such effects may be used to improve upon the performance of the naive model. An analysis of variance was carried out in order to investigate this possibility and to evaluate the systematic effects which, according to Firm A, were used in their cash management. The treatments were the 5 days of the business week; the blocks were the first, second, and third thirds of the month. Dividing the month into thirds, instead of blocking by weeks, was motivated by exploratory data analysis. The data base was divided into two parts. The set of data from the first 6 months was later used to set the parameters for all models; the set of data from the final 5 months is used to test models. Analyses of variance (ANOVs) were run with and without outliers removed.

The results are given in Table 4-2. With no outliers removed, both treatment and blocking effects are significant in the first 6 months; only the blocking is significant in the last 5 months. In general, as outliers are removed, blocking loses significance while treatments remain significant. This means that the large cash flows seem to account for the systematic effects seen in the first, second, and third parts of the month. Figure 4-3 displays the average flows for each day of the month. They may be part of the second distribution which, when pooled with the basic normal distribution, results in the fat-tailed distribution alluded to earlier. Such large flows are the most amenable to prediction on an individual basis. Even after large flows are removed and the blocking loses significance, there remains a significant systematic day-of-the-week effect in the data.

The coefficients of the treatments and blocks are listed in Table 4-3. The signs of the blocking coefficients remain the same over both time periods and over all data bases. Their magnitudes decrease as outliers are removed. None of the coefficients are significantly different from zero at significance level $\alpha = 0.01$ when subjected to t tests. However, with no outliers removed, the difference between the highest and lowest coefficients is significant at the level of significance $\alpha = 0.01$. Firm A can explain the negative coefficient in the first third of the month. A large monthly payment is made to a major supplier during this period. The other coefficients cannot be explained and in some cases are contradicted by the large inflow/outflow dates given to us by Firm A.

The signs of coefficients of the day-of-the-week effects also show stability. The magnitudes of these coefficients remain relatively large as outliers are removed. Firm A has provided no rationale for the alternating signs of these

Table 4-2
Analysis of Variance Results

Critical Values of F

† $F^4_{120} = 2.45$	$\alpha = 0.05$	
† $F^2_{120} = 3.07$	$\alpha = 0.05$	
* $F^4_{120} = 3.48$	$\alpha = 0.01$	
* $F^2_{120} = 4.79$	$\alpha = 0.01$	

Table 4-2 (cont.)

Full Data: First 6 Months

	Sum of Squares	Degrees of Freedom	Mean Square	F
Treatment	3,462,562	4	865,635	2.69†
Blocks	3,097,857	2	1,548,928	4.81*
Error	38,613,564	120	321,779	
Total − Mean	45,173,963	1		

Full Data: Second 5 Months

	Sum of Squares	Degrees of Freedom	Mean Square	F
Treatment	2,220,933	4	555,233	1.96
Blocks	2,856,403	2	1,428,201	5.05*
Error	27,388,394	97	282,354	
Total − Mean	32,465,730	1		

With 6 Outliers Removed: First 6 Months

	Sum of Squares	Degrees of Freedom	Mean Square	F
Treatment	1,483,599	4	370,599	1.56
Blocks	1,524,304	2	762,152	3.21†
Error	27,720,655	117	236,928	
Total − Mean	30,747,215	1		

With 6 Outliers Removed: Second 5 Months

	Sum of Squares	Degrees of Freedom	Mean Square	F
Treatment	2,391,618	4	597,904	3.77*
Blocks	894,329	2	247,164	1.56
Error	14,885,762	94	158,359	
Total − Mean	18,171,709	1		

With 12 Outliers Removed: First 6 Months

	Sum of Squares	Degrees of Freedom	Mean Square	F
Treatment	1,708,426	4	427,107	2.45†
Blocks	1,077,033	2	538,517	2.51
Error	19,736,375	113	174,658	
Total − Mean	22,521,834	1		

With 12 Outliers Removed: Second 5 Months

	Sum of Squares	Degrees of Freedom	Mean Square	F
Treatment	1,304,566	4	326,142	2.51†
Blocks	354,654	2	177,326	1.37
Error	11,938,532	92	129,767	
Total − Mean	13,597,750	1		

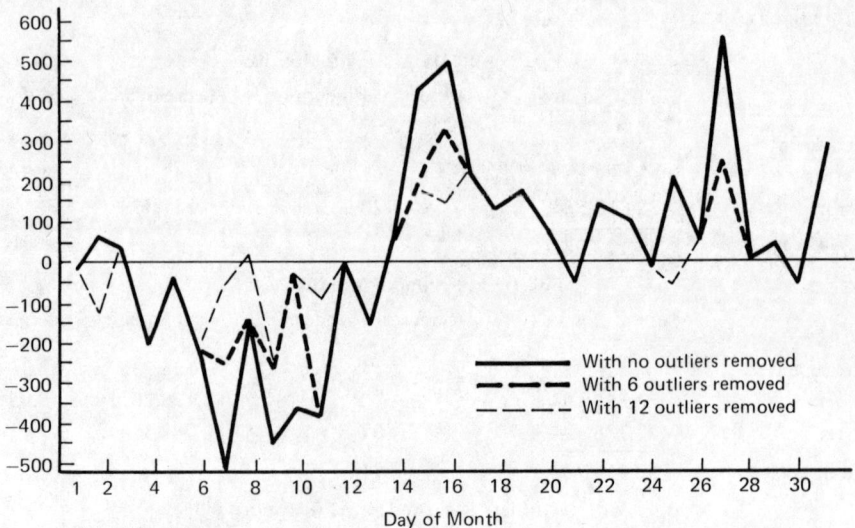

Figure 4-3. Average Daily Cash Flows by Day of the Month (in $000).

daily effects. Again the coefficients are not significantly different from zero at the level of significance $\alpha = 0.01$. However, as in the case of blocking effects, some of the coefficients are significantly different from one another.

Even though these coefficients are not significantly different from zero in the classical statistical sense, one may be able to make use of them in a strategy to improve upon the performance of a naive model. The stability of the signs might suggest the profitable use of such strategies. The benefits from such strategies depend not only on statistical significance but also on the magnitude of the related costs and benefits. One such strategy is tested by simulation in Chapter 7.

Table 4-3
Coefficients of Treatments and Blocks from Analysis of Variance

		Coefficients of Treatment (in $000)	
		First 6 Months	Last 5 Months
Full Data	Monday	−178.9	−170.9
	Tuesday	224.8	172.6
	Wednesday	−36.8	−75.5
	Thursday	174.2	187.6
	Friday	−157.4	−93.2
With 6 Outliers Removed	Monday	−85.8	−194.4
	Tuesday	147.1	261.7
	Wednesday	−16.0	−99.0
	Thursday	115.1	65.4
	Friday	−136.7	2.2
With 12 Outliers Removed	Monday	−79.9	−126.1
	Tuesday	86.6	195.3
	Wednesday	−10.2	−100.6
	Thursday	179.1	63.7
	Friday	−160.6	0.6

	Thirds of Month	Coefficients of Blocks (in $000)	
		First 6 Months	Last 5 Months
Full Data	1st	−201.6	−200.3
	2d	90.5	192.7
	3d	147.8	45.4
With 6 Outliers Removed	1st	−142.0	−114.7
	2d	59.4	110.7
	3d	109.5	21.9
With 12 Outliers Removed	1st	−126.6	−75.3
	2d	65.2	66.6
	3d	76.7	20.2

Appendix 4A

4A-1 Kolmogorov-Smirnov Test of Normality of Firm A's Daily Cash Flow Distribution—with No Outliers Removed

Net daily cash flows $= \Delta$ $N = 231$

$\bar{\Delta} = 4$ $\sigma_\Delta^2 = 338{,}589$ $\sigma_\Delta = 582$

z test on mean:

$$z = \frac{\bar{\Delta} - 0}{\sigma_\Delta / \sqrt{N}} = 0.104$$

$P(|z| > 0.104) = 2P(z > 0.104) = 0.9204$

So the mean is not significantly different from zero at $\alpha = 0.05$.

Region	Range		Events
1	$> 4\sigma$	> 2328	1
2	3σ to 4σ	1746 to 2328	2
3	2σ to 3σ	1164 to 1746	3
4	σ to 2σ	582 to 1164	20
5	0 to σ	0 to 582	86
6	$-\sigma$ to 0	-582 to 0	104
7	-2σ to $-\sigma$	-1164 to -582	9
8	-3σ to -2σ	-1746 to -1164	3
9	-4σ to -3σ	-2328 to -1746	2
10	$< -4\sigma$	< -2328	1

Region	$S_{231}(x)$ Cumulative	$F_0(x)$ Theory Cumulative	$|F_0(x) - S_{231}(x)|$
1	0.0043	0.00003	0.0043
2	0.0130	0.0013	0.0117
3	0.0260	0.0228	0.0032

(table continued next page)

Region	$S_{231}(x)$ Cumulative	$F_0(x)$ Theory Cumulative	$\|F_0(x) - S_{231}(x)\|$
4	0.1125	0.1587	0.0462
5	0.4850	0.5000	0.0150
6	0.9350	0.8413	0.0937
7	0.9750	0.9772	0.0022
8	0.9875	0.9987	0.0112
9	0.9950	1.0000	0.0050
10	1.0000	1.0000	0.0000

$$D = \max |F_0(x) - S_{231}(x)| = 0.0937$$

If

$$D > \frac{1.63}{\sqrt{N}} = \frac{1.63}{\sqrt{231}} = \frac{1.63}{15.2} = 0.107$$

then reject the hypothesis that data are from theory distributed at $\alpha = 0.01$.

Note: $D < 0.107$, so we cannot reject the hypothesis that our distribution is normal at $\alpha = 0.01$.

If

$$D > \frac{1.36}{\sqrt{N}} = \frac{1.36}{\sqrt{231}} = \frac{1.36}{15.2} = 9.0895$$

then reject the hypothesis that data are from theory distribution at $\alpha = 0.05$.

Note: $D > 0.0895$, so we must reject the hypothesis that our distribution is normal at $\alpha = 0.05$.

4A-2 Kolmogorov-Smirnov Test of Normality of Firm A's Daily Cash Flow Distribution—with 6 Outliers Removed (Minus Those Points That Are Beyond the Original 3σ Level)

Net daily cash flows $= \Delta$ $N = 225$

$$\overline{\Delta} = 3.2$$

$$\hat{\sigma}^2_{225} = \frac{49{,}000{,}000}{224} = 218{,}000$$

$$\hat{\sigma}_{225} = 466$$

z test on mean:

$$z = \frac{\overline{\Delta} - 0}{\sigma_\Delta / \sqrt{N}} = 0.103$$

$$P(|z| > 0.103) = 2P(z > 0.103) = 2(0.4602) = 0.9204$$

So the mean is not significantly different from zero.

Region	Range		Events
1	$> 3\sigma$	> 1398	3
2	2σ to 3σ	932 to 1398	6
3	σ to 2σ	466 to 932	21
4	0 to σ	0 to 466	79
5	$-\sigma$ to 0	-466 to 0	96
6	-2σ to $-\sigma$	-932 to -466	14
7	-3σ to -2σ	-1398 to -932	5
8	$< -3\sigma$	< -1398	1

Region	$S_{225}(x)$ Cumulative	$F_0(x)$ Theory Cumulative	$\|F_0(x) - S_{225}(x)\|$
1	0.0133	0.0013	0.0120
2	0.0400	0.0228	0.0172
3	0.1333	0.1587	0.0254
4	0.4850	0.5000	0.0150
5	0.9120	0.8413	0.0707
6	0.9740	0.9772	0.0032
7	0.9960	0.9987	0.0027
8	1.0000	1.0000	0.0000

$$D = \max |F_0(x) - S_{225}(x)| = 0.0707$$

If

$$D > \frac{1.63}{\sqrt{N}} = \frac{1.63}{\sqrt{225}} = \frac{1.63}{15} = 0.109$$

then reject the hypothesis that the data are from theory distribution at $\alpha = 0.01$.

If

$$D > \frac{1.36}{\sqrt{N}} = \frac{1.36}{15} = 0.0906$$

then reject the hypothesis that the data are from theory distribution at $\alpha = 0.05$.

Note: We cannot reject the hypothesis that the data are normally distributed at either $\alpha = 0.01$ or $\alpha = 0.05$.

4A-3 Kolmogorov-Smirnov Test of Normality of Firm A's Daily Cash Flow Distribution—with 12 Outliers Removed (Minus Those Points that Are Beyond the Original 2σ Level)

Net daily cash flows = Δ $N = 219$

$\overline{\Delta} = 1.0$ $\sigma_{219} = 407$

z test on mean:

$$z = \frac{\overline{\Delta} - 0}{\sigma_{\Delta}\sqrt{N}} = 0.032$$

$$P(|z| > 0.032) = 2P(z > 0.032) = 0.9760$$

Region	Range		Events
1	$> 3\sigma$	> 1221	0
2	2σ to 3σ	814 to 1221	9
3	σ to 2σ	407 to 814	23
4	0 to σ	0 to 407	74
5	$-\sigma$ to 0	-407 to 0	86
6	-2σ to $-\sigma$	-814 to -407	21
7	-3σ to -2σ	-1221 to -814	6
8	$< -3\sigma$	< -1221	0

Region	$S_{219}(x)$ Cumulative	$F_0(x)$ Theory Cumulative	$\|F_0(x) - S_{219}(x)\|$
1	0.0000	0.0013	0.0013
2	0.0411	0.0228	0.0183
3	0.1460	0.1587	0.9127
4	0.4840	0.5000	0.0160
5	0.8770	0.8413	0.0357
6	0.9730	0.9772	0.0042
7	1.0000	0.9987	0.0013
8	1.0000	1.0000	0.0000

$$D = \max |F_0(x) - S_{219}(x)| = 0.0357$$

If

$$D > \frac{1.36}{\sqrt{N}} = 0.0420$$

then reject the hypothesis that the data are from theory distribution at $\alpha = 0.05$.

If

$$D > \frac{1.22}{\sqrt{N}} = 0.0825$$

then reject the hypothesis that the data are from theory distribution at $\alpha = 0.10$.

Note: We cannot reject the hypothesis that the data are normally distributed at either $\alpha = 0.05$ or $\alpha = 0.10$.

4A-4 One Sample Runs Test on Firm A's Daily Cash Flows

```
Feb.                                                                    Mar.
| -    ++    ----++    --    +    -    +    --    +    -    ++ | +
 1     2      3   4     5    6    7    8     9   10   11    12

 -     +     -   ++    -     +   ----  +    -   ++++   -
13    14    15   16   17    18   19   20   21    22   23

             Apr.
++    --    +|+   -    +    --    +   ----  ++    -   ++++
24    25    26   27   28    29   30   31   32    33   34

             May
-----++     |    -    ++  -----+   --  ++    -    +    --
35    36         37   38   39    40   41   42   43    44   45

             June
 +   --    +|+ -----+++  --    +    -    +    --  +++
46    47   48   49   50    51   52   53   54   55   56

             July
 -   ++     -   |++ -----+    -   ++    --    +    -    +
57    58   59   60   61    62   63   64   65    66   67   68
```

```
                        Aug.
  --    +    -   ++ | -    ++    ---- +    -    +    --    +    -
  69   70   71   72   73   74    75     76   77   78   79   80   81

                             Sept.
   +    --   +    -    ++   --- | --- +    ----- ++   -    +
  82   83   84   85   86      87        88       89   90   91   92

                                        Oct.
  --   +    -    +    --   +    --   |    ++    --    +    --    +
  93   94   95   96   97   98   99         100   101   102   103   104

                                         Nov.
   -    +    --   +    -    +    --   ++++  |    -    ++
  105  106  107  108  109  110  111   112        113   114

                                        Dec.
   -    ++   -----+++++    --   ++   |    -    +    -    +
  115  116   117    118    119  120        121   122  123  124

  ----++++  -         +++  -      +         --   ++
  125  126  127   128  129   130      131   132
```

$r = 132 \qquad n_+ = N_1 = 112 \qquad n_- = N_2 = 119$

$$z = \frac{r - [2N_1 N_2 / (N_1 + N_2) + 1]}{\sqrt{\dfrac{2N_1 N_2 (2N_1 N_2 - N_1 - N_2)}{[(N_1+N_2)^2 (N_1+N_2 - 1)]}}} = \frac{16}{7.77} = 2.12$$

$P(|z \geq 2.12|) = 2P(z \geq 2.12) = 2(0.017) = 0.034$

Note: Ordering is not random at the 0.05 significance level.

4A-5 Confidence Limits of Full Distribution

Daily cash flows in $000 = x

For mean $\bar{x} \pm 2.5 S_x / \sqrt{N}$: $-\$92{,}000 < \mu < \$100{,}000$ at 99% confidence level.

$\bar{x} = \$4,000$

For variance, assuming normality,

$$\frac{S_x^2}{1 + 2.5\sqrt{2/(N-1)}} < \sigma_x^2 < \frac{S_x^2}{1 - 2.5\sqrt{2/(N-1)}}$$

$$274{,}707 \times 10^6 < \sigma^2 < 439{,}334 \times 10^6$$

$S_x^2 = 338{,}589 \times 10^6$ at 99% confidence level

4A-6 Confidence Limits on Monthly Data

For mean 99% confidence level on μ, assuming $N = 20$,

$-\$318{,}000 < \mu < \$326{,}000$. No monthly mean violates this range.

For variance using χ^2 test,

$$\frac{(N-1)S_x^2}{\chi_{0.995}^2} < \sigma^2 < \frac{(N-1)S_x^2}{\chi_{0.005}^2}$$

at 99% confidence level,

$$\$169{,}294 \times 10^6 < \sigma^2 < \$915{,}105 \times 10^6$$

Only one month, August with $S_x^2 = \$147{,}265 \times 10^6$, violates this range.

Test of mean of July (farthest from overall mean) versus full distribution without July:

$$z = \frac{\bar{x}_J - \bar{x}_{All}}{S\sqrt{\dfrac{1}{N_J} + \dfrac{1}{N_{All}}}} \quad \text{where} \quad S = \left[\frac{(N_J - 1)S_J^2 + (N_{All} - 1)S_{All}^2}{N_J + N_{All} - 2}\right]^{1/2}$$

$z = 0.96$

The two means are not significantly different.

Test of mean of July (largest positive mean) versus mean of September (largest negative mean):

$z = 0.94$

The two means are not significantly different.

Test of variance of July (largest monthly variance) versus variance of full distribution with July deleted:

$$F^{20}_{211} = \frac{S_J^2}{S^2_{All}} = 2.61$$

The variances are not significantly different at $\alpha = 0.05$.

Test of variance of August (smallest monthly variance) versus variance of full distribution with August deleted:

$$F^{210}_{21} = \frac{S^2_{All}}{S^2_{Aug}} = 2.51$$

The variances are significantly different at $\alpha = 0.05$.

Test of July versus August variances:

$$F^{20}_{21} = \frac{S^2_J}{S^2_{Aug}} = 4.74$$

The variances are significantly different at $\alpha = 0.01$ level of significance.

Stability of monthly means remains after outliers are deleted. However, confidence limits on monthly variances with 12 outliers removed are violated in the case of September.

$$82{,}860 \times 10^6 < \sigma^2 < 473{,}490 \times 10^6$$

99% confidence limits

September: $S^2 = 67{,}794 \times 10^6$

With 12 outliers removed, the largest monthly variance, December's, is not significantly different at the $\alpha = 0.01$ level from the overall variance with December deleted.

$$F^{22}_{195} = \frac{S^2_{Dec}}{S^2_{All}} = 1.65 \quad \text{not significant at } \alpha = 0.01 \text{ level}$$

With 12 outliers removed, comparing the largest monthly variance (December) with the smallest (September) yields

$$F^{22}_{20} = 2.57$$

The variances are not significantly different at $\alpha = 0.05$, but they are significantly different at $\alpha = 0.01$.

5 Decision Models with an Absolute Minimum Cash Balance Constraint

5-1 Introduction

This chapter develops analytical control limit models for liquid asset management with an absolute minimum cash balance constraint. Measures for evaluating model performance are developed and applied to several of these models.

The beginning of this chapter summarizes the original Miller-Orr two-asset model (Miller and Orr, 1966) and Orr's three-asset model (Orr, 1970). Some assumptions of these models are questioned, motivating extensions of the modeling effort.

A general three-asset simulation model is described, with a discussion about its use in testing the performance of analytical decision rules on real data from Firm A. The first application of the simulation model is an experiment to find Firm A's implicit transaction costs.

Modeling extensions of the inventory control approach are developed, and their performance is measured by the simulation model. The first extension is a two-asset model which allows different transaction costs for buying and selling securities. Next is a model which allows the firm to issue debt itself as an alternative to selling earning assets prematurely whenever it experiences a cash shortage. Last, there is a comparison between a four-asset and a five-asset model which automatically "flip over" the three-asset Orr model when the firm goes into a net borrowing position.

5-2 The Miller-Orr Two-asset Model

The Miller-Orr model is an inventory control model concerned with two assets—cash and an interest-bearing security. The cash balance is the item subject to control under the following assumptions:

1. There is an absolute minimum level of cash which must be held as bank deposits.
2. The opportunity cost of holding cash is linear in the amount of cash held and in the length of time that it is held. The opportunity cost is equal to the interest foregone by holding cash rather than the highest yielding earning asset available.
3. The cost per transaction of converting cash to earning assets, or vice versa, is independent of the size and direction of the transfer.

4. Daily cash flows are the sum of many Bernoulli-distributed flows. The resulting distribution of daily cash flows is normally distributed with a mean zero and a variance σ^2.
5. The earning assets have an infinite lifetime (i.e., there is no "runoff").
6. All transactions take place virtually instantaneously.
7. The portfolio of assets is adjusted, at most, once per day.

The last assumption (item 7) is not present in the Miller-Orr formulation but is included here so that the resulting model conforms to customary business practice.

Recall that the simple Miller-Orr (h,z) control policy allows the cash balance M to fluctuate randomly between a lower bound M_L and an upper bound M_U. Whenever the cash balance violates one of these boundaries, the cash balance is returned to a level $M_L + z$ through the purchase or sale of securities. The range over which the cash balance fluctuates is $h = M_U - M_L$. The absolute minimum cash balance level M_L is the firm's compensating-balance requirement and is externally determined. The variables h and z are chosen to minimize expected daily costs.

The expected daily cost $E(C)$ consists of both the expected daily transaction costs caused by the purchase and sale of securities and the expected daily opportunity costs due to holding cash. The expected daily transaction cost equals the product of the cost per transaction b and the probability of a transaction in any given day $P(T)$. The expected daily opportunity cost equals the product of the daily (average) interest rate i of a security and the expected cash balance $E(M)$.

$$\min_{h,z} E(C) = b \frac{\sigma^2}{z(h-z)} + M_L i + \frac{h+z}{3} i$$

Appendix 5A shows how the minimization of expected costs may be restated in terms of the decision variables.

The first-order conditions for a minimum $E(C)$[a] [that is, $\dfrac{\partial E(C)}{\partial z} = \dfrac{\partial E(C)}{\partial h} = 0$] yield

$$h_{opt} = 3 z_{opt} \qquad z_{opt} = \left(\frac{3b\sigma^2}{4i}\right)^{1/3}$$

Note that a more explicit expression for $P(T)$ is

$$P(T) = \min\left[\frac{\sigma^2}{z(h-z)}, 1.0\right]$$

---

[a]The minimum $E(C)$ and its response to changes in b, i, and σ are given in Appendix 5B.

If $P(T)$ were to exceed 1.0, it would imply that the firm must make more than one transaction per day. The assumptions of the model exclude such a possibility. $P(T) = 1.0$ when

$$\frac{\sigma^2}{z_{opt}(h_{opt} - z_{opt})} \geq 1.0$$

or

$$\frac{\sigma i}{b} \geq 3.78$$

Under this condition the objective function $E(C)$ becomes

$$\min_{z,h} E(C) = b + \left(M_L + \frac{h+z}{3}\right)i$$

and the first-order conditions yield

$$h_{opt} = z_{opt} = 0$$

Hence, the cash balance is adjusted to M_L every day. This policy is a special case of a linear adjustment model which is discussed in Chapter 8.

With Firm A's cash flow characteristics, an assumed transaction cost of $30, a yearly interest rate of 5-7/8%, and no compensating-balance requirement, the model yields a hypothetical h of $774,000, a z of $258,000, and a mean cash balance of $344,000. This means that Firm A's compensating-balance constraint of $3 million requires the firm to maintain an additional $2,656,000 in demand deposits beyond the transaction demand. If we assume an opportunity earnings rate of 5-7/8%, this results in $156,040 of lost interest earnings annually.

This basic Miller-Orr approach is most relevant for the small or medium-sized firm. For larger firms, transaction costs are relatively insignificant in cash management when compared with interest revenues flowing from the firms' large cash balances. Furthermore, for a variety of reasons, larger firms must allocate managerial resources to dealing in the financial markets. Hence, in terms of managerial time, the incremental cost of making transactions is rather small. Often, in smaller firms, managerial resources are allocated to money-market operations for the sole purpose of investing idle cash balances. Hence, systematic methods which routinize cash management can result in real savings of managerial time and effort.

5-3 Orr's Three-asset Model

Firm A utilizes two earning assets: RPs and CDs. The RP inventory buffers the CD inventory from daily demands for cash. RPs mature in 1 day and have a lower interest rate than CDs. Furthermore, the firm incurs a purchase and a "runoff" transaction cost for each day that it maintains a positive RP balance. Hence, Firm A is willing to forego some interest revenue and incur some transaction costs by maintaining a balance of low-yield, but highly liquid, securities in order to avoid the cost of prematurely selling high-yield securities. Since Firm A makes its cash management decisions within a three-asset framework, the following three-asset analytical model is used in Section 5-6 to arrive at its implicit costs per transaction for each of the earning assets.

Orr (1970) assumes three-asset balances: cash M, short-term securities S, and long-term securities L. His model places control limits with single return points on two assets: M_L, $M_L + z$, and $M_L + h$ for cash balance M; and $0, Z$, and H for "short" balance S. Orr proves that, under these control rules, changes in the "short" balance S have the same variance, σ^2, as the net cash flows and that the "short" balance performs a random walk over the $(0,H)$ region. This fact allows Orr to separate the management of the cash from that of the short balance into two Miller-Orr problems.

The composite objective function (the sum of the two separate objective functions) is

$$\min_{z,h,Z,H} E(C) = b_S \frac{\sigma^2}{z(h-z)} + i_L \frac{h+z}{3} + i_L M_L + b_L \frac{\sigma^2}{Z(H-Z)}$$

$$+ (i_L - i_S) \frac{H+Z}{3}$$

where

b_S, b_L = the costs per transaction of "shorts" and "longs," respectively

i_S, i_L = the daily interest rates of "shorts" and "longs," respectively.

The optimal control parameters are

$$h_{opt} = 3 z_{opt} \qquad H_{opt} = 3 Z_{opt}$$

$$z_{opt} = \left(\frac{3 b_S \sigma^2}{4 i_L}\right)^{1/3} \qquad Z_{opt} = \left[\frac{3 b_L \sigma^2}{4(i_L - i_S)}\right]^{1/3}$$

5-4 The Need for Extension of the Miller-Orr Model

The Miller-Orr model is an idealization of the real world. As such, it cannot handle some characteristics of the debt markets and certain features of daily cash flows. Although Miller, Orr, and other researchers[b] have found the Miller-Orr model to be robust, some of the model's omissions are stated in this section. In the rest of this chapter and subsequent chapters, extensions of the Miller-Orr model are developed to confront some of the following issues.

(1) *The costs of buying and selling securities are not equal.* The 120-day certificate of deposit (CD) is a likely candidate for a "long" earning asset. It is safe and costs very little to purchase from an issuing bank. However, selling it is more costly. If the CD does not have a secondary market, the holder can sell it back to the issuing bank and will incur a "goodwill cost"; the sale may complicate bank-firm relationships. If the CD does have a secondary market, then the seller will pay to the specialist a spread of approximately 5 basis points (that is, 5/100 of 1% of the value of the CD). For example, 5 basis points on a $1,000,000 CD is $500. On occasion, the spread becomes as large as 15 basis points. This criticism is relevant for another most likely candidate for a "long" earning asset, the treasury bill.

(2) *Returns on assets are a function of how long they are held.* Orr's three-asset model considers two daily interest rates for "longs" and "shorts," but one would expect that a "long" held only 1 day before being sold should earn no more than a 1-day repurchase agreement (RP) held to maturity. In fact, one might expect to see the following form of relationship between the daily interest rate i_n and the number of days, n, that a security is held:

$$i_n = A + B(1 - e^{-an})$$

where A, B, and a are all positive. The Miller-Orr model assumes that the daily interest rate is independent of how long a security is held.

(3) *The firm may wish to issue debt to cover transactions demand.* There are two possible reasons for this kind of transactions demand borrowing. First, the firm may find that the transaction cost of issuing short-term debt or borrowing on a line of credit is less expensive than discounting a "long." Second, the firm may go into a period in which it has a negative liquid asset balance or a liquid asset balance that is less than its compensating-balance requirements. Of course, the debt which is issued will probably have a higher interest rate than that of securities which the firm has been buying on its "cash-rich" days.

(4) *The securities may mature before being sold.* The Miller-Orr model assumes that a maturity either has an infinite maturity date or conveniently

---

[b]Eppen and Fama (1968) have shown that the Miller-Orr model gives reasonable solutions even when transaction costs are proportional to the amount transferred.

comes due on the day which the decision model indicates a sale. Actually, the decisionmaker must deal with maturation (or "runoff") costs and cash inflows caused by securities coming due.[c]

(5) *The net cash inflows may have systematic effects.* If the decisionmaker can anticipate daily, weekly, and seasonal effects, there is an opportunity to improve upon the performance of the pure model. Furthermore, if the decisionmaker can forecast specific large flows, it might be possible to reduce the costs of dealing with them.

(6) *The bank may specify another form of compensating-balance constraint.* There are a number of possible forms of compensating-balance constraints. Although the Miller-Orr model assumes an absolute minimum cash balance, in Chapter 6 we develop a model with the more common restriction, a minimum average cash balance, and a linear penalty function for violating the minimum. Frost (1970) has discussed the relationship between the provision of bank services to a firm and its compensating balance.[d]

5-5 Simulation as a Test of the Models

A general three-asset computer simulation model was developed to test the utility of the models presented in Chapters 5 and 6. The structure and versatility of such a model for corporate decisionmaking are discussed in Chapter 7. In this chapter, decisions in accordance with control rules indicated by various analytical models are applied to actual data supplied by Firm A. The data, described in Chapter 4, cover the period from February 2, 1971 to December 31, 1971.

The appropriate measure of effectiveness for the various decision rules is net average daily profit (i.e., average daily interest revenue minus average daily transaction costs). Fortunately, this measure is highly quantifiable; however, the transaction costs include some fuzzy cost elements such as managerial time and loss of goodwill. The average used here is defined over business days, not calendar days.

Sound methodology dictates that information about future events which is not available to a manager at the time of a decision must not be made available to the models. The data from Firm A on the 231 business days are split into two parts. The first 127 business days (February 2 to July 31) are used to set the parameters of the models. The next 104 business days (August 2 to December

---

[c]Although "runoffs" present problems to the cash manager, they are not included in the statistical analysis of Firm A's daily cash flow in Chapter 4. In that chapter, daily cash flows consist only of daily changes in the total liquid asset balance of the firm.

[d]Frost (1970) argues that banks value the cash deposits which are above an absolute minimum cash balance constraint (and, therefore, display variance) less than the deposits which are required to remain stable by the compensating-balance agreement. He claims the amount of services provided by a bank to its client depends on the total value of these two types of deposits.

31) are used to test the effectiveness of the parameterized models. This procedure divides the 11 months of data roughly in half while maintaining integral months. This division causes no problems in terms of seasonality since in Chapter 4 we indicated that there are no obvious seasonal effects in the cash flow data.

The model uses interest rates that are appropriate to the period in question. During the period of investigation the effective annual interest rate on 120-day CDs was 5-7/8% and the annual rate on RPs was 5-1/8%. The firm felt that it could borrow at an annual rate of 1% above the CD rate (that is, 6-7/8%). Since some of the models indicate selling earning assets before maturity, it is important to approximate the yield curve from 1 to 120 days. The simulation model uses an approximation with a linear relationship between the daily interest rate and the amount of time that an asset is held. That is,

i_L = the daily interest rate of a CD held the full 120 days

$= (1 + 0.05875)^{1/365} - 1$

i_S = the daily interest rate of an RP or a CD held 1 day[e]

$= (1 + 0.05125)^{1/365} - 1$

i_n = the daily interest rate of a CD held n days

$= i_S + \dfrac{(n-1)(i_L - i_S)}{119}$ where $1 \leq n \leq 120$

The accumulated interest on a CD held exactly n days is $(1 + i_n)^n - 1$. This linear yield curve understates interest rates of the intermediate maturities as compared with the convex yield curve often observed.

Furthermore, the simulation model uses a LIFO (Last In, First Out) procedure for choosing which securities to sell when the cash balance falls to M_L. Those securities which are not sold before maturity produce a cash influx at maturity and cause a maturation or "runoff" cost.

In addition to the profit performance, the simulation model prints out other data about the simulated activity of the firm. A table displays all possible daily transaction events (e.g., an RP came due, an RP was bought, and a CD was bought) and lists for how many days each combination of events occurred. The averages and standard deviations of the cash balance, of the RP balance, and of the CD balance are shown. The average and standard deviation of days between sales of "longs" are printed out, as is the interest accrued from the two earning

---

[e]RPs are sold at a discount, and their interest rates are computed on a 360-day basis. Although the simulation model does not compute RP interest in this manner, an adjustment of the computation method would not significantly change the model's performance.

assets. Last, the summary statistics give the average daily interest revenue, average daily transaction cost, and average daily profit from the use of the specified decision rule.[f]

5-6 Examples of the Application of the Simulation Model

The simulation model was used to obtain a rough estimate of the implicit costs per transaction for Firm A. The approach followed was to calculate the control limits of the three-asset Orr model, varying the two costs per transaction, and to simulate the results of these limits until the model "replicated" the behavior of Firm A over the 11-month period. The behavior chosen for replication was the number of days with no transactions (62), the total number of buys, sells, and runoffs of CDs (39), and the number of days on which RPs were purchased (149). The simulation used the 11-month estimated standard deviation of daily cash flow s_m = \$583,000, the interest annual rate of the period (I_L = 5-7/8%, I_S = 5-1/8%), 120-day CDs, the Firm's minimum average compensating-balance requirement[g] $\overline{M}^*$ = \$3 million, and the two cost-per-transaction charges b_S and b_L, which were each varied from \$0.50 to \$45. The simulation model came closest to replicating Firm A's behavior when b_L = \$15 and b_S = \$2. These implicit costs are close to the \$0-to-\$10 range estimated by the Firm. While Firm A's implicit transaction costs are consistent with its actions, these values do not necessarily reflect the "true" transaction costs.

Table 5-1 displays the 11-month average balances[h] (designated by an overbar)

**Table 5-1
An 11-Month Three-asset Simulation Using Firm A's Implicit Costs per Transaction**

	$\overline{M}$	s_M	$\overline{RP}$	s_{RP}	$\overline{CD}$	s_{CD}
Firm A	\$3,567,700	\$839,000	\$924,700	\$969,500	\$3,686,900	\$1,700,000
Orr Model	\$2,969,000	\$ 77,000	\$467,000	\$464,000	\$4,764,000	\$1,858,000

---

[f]These averages are defined over business days, not calendar days.

[g]The simulation model which was used to determine implicit values of b_S and b_L has a minimum average compensating-balance constraint rather than an absolute minimum cash balance constraint. The analytical model which was used to determine the control limits is the three-asset version of the adjusted, symmetric transaction cost Miller-Orr model discussed in Section 6-4.

[h]At the time this simulation was performed, there were several errors in the data. These errors tended to increase $\overline{M} + \overline{RP} + \overline{CD}$ above its appropriate level. These errors were removed from the data for all the other simulations reported in this book.

and the standard deviations (designated by s) of the three assets both for Firm A and for the simulation model using b_L = $15 and b_S = $2. There are two important points in Table 5-1. The Orr model keeps the average cash balance $\overline{M}$ considerably closer to the minimum average compensating balance $\overline{M}^*$ = $3 million than does Firm A, while the variance of the cash balance s_M^2 is reduced. Furthermore, the model shifts more of the liquid assets into high-yield CDs rather than into RPs. However, an important caveat must be given with respect to Table 5-1: the simulation model assumes symmetric costs per transaction while the cash managers at Firm A know that this is not the case.

In the rest of this chapter and in Chapter 6, seven simulations are presented which show the results of seven varieties of control limit models applied to Firm A's data. The method of testing these models is the same in each case. The data from the first 127 business days (from February 1971 through July 1971) is used to set the parameters of the models. The resultant control limits are then used for the simulation of decision and accounting processes on data from the next 104 business days (from August 1971 through December 1971). The estimated standard deviation of net daily cash flows from the first 6 months s_M is $597,000. The total cash and securities balance on July 31, 1971 was $11,726,000; all assets are assumed to be cash on the first day of the simulation. "Long" interest bearing assets (for example, CDs and CPs) mature in 119 days. Each simulation is run with the cost per "buy" transaction b set to four values: $10, $30, $50, and $70. Although Firm A actually had a minimum average cash balance constraint, a surrogate absolute minimum cash balance constraint is constructed for these simulations by choosing M_L such that Firm A's cash balance falls below M_L only 5% of the 231 business days. The resulting absolute minimum balance M_L is $2,300,000.

The actual performance of Firm A is presented with the results of each of the seven simulations. However, direct comparisons between Firm A and the models are sometimes misleading. Firm A's results are presented side by side with the model's results as much to show where comparisons are inappropriate as to study them when they are appropriate. Firm A's interest revenue for the August-to-December period excludes interest accrued before August but reported during the 5-month period, and includes interest accrued during the period and reported after December.[i] During the last 5 months of the 11-month

---

[i]The following is a calculation of the estimated interest revenue accrued by Firm A between August 2, 1971 and December 31, 1971.

Interest collected between August 2 and December 31	$133,900
− Interest accrued prior to August 2 but realized after August 2 (estimate)	−45,570
+ Interest accrued between August 2 and December 31 but not realized until 1972 (estimate)	+40,380
Interest accrued between August 2 and December 31 (estimate)	$129,710

Hence, the average interest revenue accrued by Firm A on a business day between August 2 and December 31 is $129,710/104 = $1,247.20.

period, Firm A executed transactions on 80 days (ignoring RP runoffs). RPs were purchased on 79 days, CDs were purchased on 7 days, and CDs matured on 8 days. In the tables of results of simulations, the column representing Firm A's results assumes that Firm A incurs a transaction cost of b dollars on each day that the firm executes one of the above transactions. Hence, the transaction cost incurred by Firm A over the last 5 months of the period was $\$80 \times b$, and the average transaction cost per business day was $(\$80 \times b)/104$, or $\$0.77 \times b$.

Table 5-2 shows the results of the first simulation in the series of seven. The analytical model used in the simulation is the two-asset symmetric transaction cost Miller-Orr model. The profit performance of the model appears to surpass that of Firm A for each value of b that was used. The model is able to maintain a lower average cash balance than Firm A and places the excess assets in high-yield CDs. However, the model ignores and violates Firm A's minimum average cash

Table 5-2
Two-asset Symmetric Transaction Cost Miller-Orr Model with Absolute Minimum Cash Constraint

	Results of 104-day Simulation Compared with Firm A's Actual Results				
	Two-asset Model				Firm A
b (in \$)	10	30	50	70	–
M_L (in \$000)	2,300	2,300	2,300	2,300	–
z (in \$000)	258	372	440	493	–
h (in \$000)	774	1,116	1,320	1,479	–
$\overline{M}$ (in \$000)	2,636	2,770	2,796	2,884	3,098
S_M (in \$000)	170	246	280	342	642
$\overline{RP}$ (in \$000)	–	–	–	–	1,002
S_{RP} (in \$000)	–	–	–	–	972
$\overline{CD}$ (in \$000)	6,149	6,014	5,988	5,900	4,684
S_{CD} (in \$000)	1,662	1,659	1,709	1,729	1,769
Number of CD transactions	39	30	23	18	15
Number of RP buys	–	–	–	–	79
Number of transaction days	39	30	23	18	80
Average daily interest revenue (in \$ per day)	1,340.1	1,313.6	1,306.3	1,287.1	1,247.2
Average daily transaction cost (in \$ per day)	3.7	8.7	11.1	12.1	$0.77 \times b$
Average daily profit (in \$ per day)	1,336.3	1,304.9	1,295.2	1,275.0	–
Firm A's average daily profit (in \$ per day)	1,239.5	1,224.1	1,208.7	1,193.4	

balance constraint. Furthermore, the model does not consider the possibility of large goodwill costs and does not spread costs associated with selling "longs" before maturity. One point that is worthy of comparison is that the cash balance variance of the model is significantly lower than that of Firm A. If a bank is willing to reward low variance in cash balances, then a variation of the model may be of value in negotiations for increased bank services or for lower compensating-balance requirements.

5-7 The Two-asset Asymmetric Transaction Cost Model

The Miller-Orr model assumes equal transaction costs for transfers into and out of earning assets. However, most earning assets are sold at significant discounts (5 basis points) in secondary markets. Firm A recognizes this large charge for selling CDs and maintains a buffer of RPs to avoid selling CDs. This discount is especially significant to the small and medium-sized firms for which the Miller-Orr model is relevant. In this section the basic Miller-Orr approach is extended to handle this aspect of the business environment.

The two-asset assymetric transaction cost model with an absolute minimum cash balance constraint is almost identical to the two-asset Miller-Orr model described in Section 5-2. However, the expected daily transaction cost consists of two terms: the expected daily cost of purchasing earning assets and the expected daily cost of selling earning assets. The minimization problem is stated as follows:

$$\min_{z,h} E(C) = b_h P(T_h) + b_o P(T_o) + iE(M)$$

where

b_h, b_o = the cost per transaction of a "buy" and a "sell" of the earning asset, respectively

$P(T_h), P(T_o)$ = the probability of a "buy" transaction and a "sell" transaction on a given day, respectively.

Appendix 5A, Section 5A-2, shows that in the steady-state, the minimization problem is restated as

$$\min_{z,h} E(C) = \frac{\sigma^2}{h}\left(\frac{b_h}{h-z} + \frac{b_o}{z}\right) + i\frac{h+z}{3} + iM_L$$

The first-order conditions for the minimization of $E(C)$ lead to a cubic equation in z and $h - z$. This equation can be solved by standard analytic techniques and will yield one real root and two conjugate imaginary roots if $b_0 > b_h$. Since it costs more to sell a security than to buy it, the condition is met and leads to the following solution:[j]

$$h_{opt} = (1 + A)z_{opt}$$

$$A = \left\{ \frac{b_h}{b_0} \left[1 + \left(1 - \frac{b_h}{b_0}\right)^{1/2} \right] \right\}^{1/3}$$

$$+ \left\{ \frac{b_h}{b_0} \left[1 - \left(1 - \frac{b_h}{b_0}\right)^{1/2} \right] \right\}^{1/3}$$

$$z_{opt} = \left[\frac{3}{i} \sigma^2 \frac{b_h(1 + 2A) + b_0 A^2}{A^2(1 + A)^2} \right]^{1/3}$$

Note that A will range between 0 and 2 for all $b_0 > b_h$. When $b_0 = b_h$, the solution reduces to that of the two-asset Miller-Orr model described in Section 5-2.

As in the previous section, the set of data supplied by Firm A is split into a 6-month and a 5-month section. The first part of the data is used to set the parameters of the model; the second part is used for the simulation of cash management decisions. The interest-bearing securities used in this simulation are 119-day CDs.

The decisionmaker may use either objective or subjective values for b_0 and b_h, whichever appears to be appropriate in that case. For this simulation, b_0, the cost per transaction of selling a CD, is assumed to consist of the normal cost per transaction, b_h, plus the 5-basis-point spread for the dealer. The spread cost is a "proportional" cost; therefore, b_0 depends upon z_{opt}. Since the asymmetric Miller-Orr model assumes strictly "lumpy" transaction charges, an effective "lumpy" value for b_0 is approximated by the following iterative procedure:

1. Set $b_0^{(1)}$ equal to b_h.
2. Compute z_{opt} according to the preceding formulas.
3. Recompute $b_0^{(2)} = b_h + 0.0005 z_{opt}$.
4. Reiterate through steps 2 and 3.

---

[j]Weitzman (1968) approached the asymmetric case in a fashion similar to the formulation presented here. While he solved the equations for several special cases, he did not report the more complete solution shown in our text. The authors are grateful for the help that they received from Prof. Warren Hausman in arriving at the analytical solution.

In all cases where this procedure was used, b_0 converged at the second decimal point by the twentieth iteration. Table 5-3 shows the results of this iterative procedure, using the data from the first 127 business days and using four values for b_h: $10, $30, $50, and $70.

The resultant values of b_h, b_0, z_{opt} are used in the simulation model for the last 104 business days. The results, reported in Table 5-4, show that for the above control limits the average cash balances of the asymmetric model are both higher than that of Firm A and also higher than those of the symmetric transaction cost model. The average cash balances increase since z_{opt}, h_{opt} and, therefore, $(h_{opt} + z_{opt})/3$ are increased to avoid the high b_0 costs, while M_L remains fixed. Firm A, on the other hand, protects itself from high b_0 costs by maintaining a buffer of RPs. Naturally, the symmetric transaction cost model did not have a high b_0 cost to avoid.

5-8 The "Matched Loading" Model

This section offers an alternative solution to dealing with asymmetric transaction costs.[k] This approach avoids the high transaction cost of prematurely selling earning assets A by issuing short-term debt D (or borrowing against a line of credit) on days when the cash balance drops below the minimum cash balance constraint M_L.

Several assumptions must be added to the formulation developed in Section 5-7. First, the cost per transaction b of a firm's selling (issuing) its own debt is assumed to be no different than the cost of buying earning assets once the firm has set up the arrangements for selling short-term debt on a regular basis. Second, the daily interest rate i_D that a firm must pay for its own debt is greater than the daily interest rate i_A that it would receive on the relatively safe earning assets that it buys for its portfolio. For example, if the firm buys CDs from a bank and issues CPs itself, the difference in interest rates is a risk premium.

The "matched loading" model divides time into fixed planning periods of

Table 5-3
Results of the Iterative Computation of b_0 for Use in the Two-asset Asymmetric Transaction Cost Model

b_h ($)	10	30	50	70
b_0 ($)	767	736	733	740
z_{opt} ($000)	1,514	1,411	1,365	1,340
A (units)	0.340	0.527	0.645	0.736
h_{opt} ($000)	2,030	2,160	2,245	2,325

---

[k]Firm A's cash management policy focuses on this issue. RPs are used as a buffer to avoid discounting CDs.

Table 5-4
Two-asset Asymmetric Transaction Cost Miller-Orr Model with Absolute Minimum Cash Constraint

	Result of 104-day Simulation Compared with Firm A's Actual Results				
	Two-asset Model				Firm A
b_h (buy) (in $)	10	30	50	70	–
b_o (sell) (in $)	767	736	733	740	–
M_L (in $000)	2,300	2,300	2,300	2,300	–
z (in $000)	1,514	1,411	1,365	1,340	–
h (in $000)	2,029	2,159	2,252	2,332	–
$\overline{M}$ (in $000)	3,412	3,345	3,311	3,397	3,098
S_M (in $000)	476	496	516	614	642
$\overline{RP}$ (in $000)	–	–	–	–	1,002
S_{RP} (in $000)	–	–	–	–	972
$\overline{CD}$ (in $000)	5,373	5,439	5,473	5,387	4,684
S_{CD} (in $000)	1,811	1,812	1,824	1,904	1,769
Number of CD transactions	12	12	12	11	15
Number of RP buys	–	–	–	–	79
Number of transaction days	12	12	12	11	80
Average daily interest revenue (in $ per day)	1,161.5	1,179.9	1,182.6	1,165.6	1,247.2
Average daily CD (buy + runoff) + RP transaction cost (in $ per day)	0.8	2.0	3.4	4.0	$0.77 \times b$
Average daily sell transaction cost (in $ per day)	29.5	35.4	35.2	35.6	–
Average daily profit (in $ per day)	1,131.2	1,142.5	1,144.1	1,125.9	–
Firm A's average daily profit (in $ per day)	1,239.5	1,224.1	1,208.7	1,193.4	

N-day duration. Within this planning period, assets are purchased on days when the cash balance exceeds M_U (that is, $M_L + h$), and debt is issued and sold on days when the cash balance falls to M_L. On these days, adjustments return the cash balance to $M_L + z$. Hence, the cash balance M in this formulation behaves just as it does in the earlier models. However, an important difference in this model is that the assets and debt are chosen so that they all mature on the last day of the planning periods.[1] That is, all securities are "loaded" onto 1 day. For

---
[1] If the decisionmaker can predict the data and size of large future inflows or outflows, the maturity date of the assets or debt can be set to coincide with those occasions. Although it is not necessary to have the maturity dates of assets and liabilities coincide with each other, this "matching" saves transaction costs.

example, if the planning period runs from January 1 to February 1, then a CD bought on January 3 and a CP issued on January 17 would both mature on February 1. On the last day of the period, the firm incurs a maturation cost which is assigned a value b_M.

The objective function is stated in terms of minimizing the expected costs $E_N(C)$ over the N-day planning period and $E_N(C) = NE(C)$.

$$\min_{z,h} E_N(C) = E_N \text{ (transaction costs of buying and issuing securities)}$$
$$+ E_N \text{ (opportunity cost of holding cash rather than retiring debt)}$$
$$+ E_N \text{ (opportunity cost of holding low-yield assets } A \text{ rather than retiring high-interest debt } D)$$
$$+ E \text{ (maturation costs)}$$

The third term on the right-hand side of the equation requires some explanation. The last day of one planning period initializes the next period. The cash and the assets and liabilities are netted out, and if the resultant balance violates the control limits, the appropriate transaction returns the cash balance to the return point $M_L + z$ On subsequent days, the expected daily increment Δ to the earning asset balance equals the expected daily increment to the debt balance. From Appendix 5A, Section 5A-2,

$$\Delta = (h-z)P(T_h) = zP(T_0) = \frac{\sigma^2}{h}$$

So, on the average both asset and debt balances are growing at an equal and linear rate. The cumulation of earning asset balance $E_N(A)$ on the Nth (or last) day of the planning period exclusive of the initialized balance is

$$F_N(A) = \sum_{n=1}^{N} n\Delta = \frac{N(N+1)}{2}\Delta = \frac{N(N+1)}{2}\frac{\sigma^2}{h}$$

The expected N-day opportunity cost of holding these assets instead of applying them to reduce the "mirror image" debt balance is the product of the difference in the two interest rates times $F_N(A)$. The minimization of $E_N(C)$ becomes

$$\min_{z,h} E_N(C) = NbP(T) + Ni_A E(M) + (i_L - i_A)F_N(A) + b_M$$

Restating this equation in terms of policy variables and expressing the objective function as the minimum expected daily cost:

$$\min_{z,h} E(C) = \min_{z,h} \frac{E_N(C)}{N}$$

$$= \frac{b\sigma^2}{(h-z)z} + i_A \frac{h+z}{3} + i_A M_L + (i_D - i_A)\frac{\sigma^2(N+1)}{2h} + \frac{b_M}{N}$$

Unfortunately, this minimization problem is not amenable to simple analytical solutions of the first-order conditions. However, the optimal policy variables may be approximated, for a specific set of parameters, by varying the policy variables and choosing those values which lead to the smallest evaluated objective function from the sample.

This procedure is carried out for the parameters of the first 127 business days of Firm A data. The yearly interest rate of debt suggested by Firm A is 6-7/8%, which is 1% higher than the yearly CD rate. The maturation cost b_M is arbitrarily chosen to equal b, the cost per transaction. Note that the value of b_M should not alter the choice of z_{opt} or h_{opt}; however, it would alter the optimal value of N if one were seeking it.

Table 5-5 shows the approximate optimal solutions to the matched loading equation with various values for N and b_0. The table consists of doublets (z_{opt}, r) where $r = h_{opt}/z_{opt}$. These solutions were found by varying z from $20,000 to $10,000,000 in increments of $20,000 and by varying r from 1 to 4 in increments of 0.1. Note that $r = 3.1 \pm 0.1$ and this value is very close to $r = 3$ for the standard two-asset Miller-Orr model. Furthermore, the values of z_{opt} are within 10% of the standard Miller-Orr model calculated in Section 5-6.

The optimal control limits reported in Table 5-5 (with $N = 119$) are used in a simulation of the matched loading model on Firm A's last 104 business days. A comparison of the matched loading model with the asymmetric transaction cost

Table 5-5
Solutions to the Matched Loading Control Limits for Different Costs per Transaction (b) and Different Planning Period Lengths (N)

		Cost per Transaction b ($)			
		10	30	50	70
Length of Planning Period N (Days)	119	240,000[a] 3.3[b]	360,000 3.1	420,000 3.1	480,000 3.0
	56	260,000 3.1	360,000 3.1	440,000 3.1	480,000 3.1
	28	260,000 3.1	360,000 3.1	440,000 3.0	480,000 3.1
	14	260,000 3.1	360,000 3.1	440,000 3.0	480,000 3.1
	7	260,000 3.1	360,000 3.1	440,000 3.0	480,000 3.1

[a]The first element in each table entry is z_{opt} (in $).
[b]The second element in each table entry is $r = h_{opt}/z_{opt}$.

model in Section 5-7 shows that the former produced a much lower average daily transaction cost. However, the profit in Table 5-6 exceeds the profit in Table 5-4 mainly because the matched loading model can maintain a lower average cash balance $\bar{M}$. This lower balance results in higher interest revenue. Although Firm A performs almost as well as the matched loading model, a comparison of the two is misleading since the model ignores and violates Firm A's banking constraint on average cash balances.

Table 5-6
Matched Loading Model with Absolute Minimum Cash Constraint

	Results of 104-day Simulation Compared with Firm A's Actual Results				
	Matched Loading Model				Firm A
b (in $)	10	30	50	70	–
M_L (in $000)	2,300	2,300	2,300	2,300	–
z (in $000)	240	360	420	480	–
M_U (in $000)	3,092	3,416	3,602	3,740	–
$\bar{M}$ (in $000)	2,650	2,765	2,776	2,840	3,098
S_M (in $000)	182	237	278	321	642
$\overline{RP}$ (in $000)	–	–	–	–	1,002
S_{RP} (in $000)	–	–	–	–	972
$\overline{CD}$ (in $000)	10,964	10,847	10,209	10,108	4,684
S_{CD} (in $000)	3,439	3,454	3,001	3,048	1,769
$\overline{CP}$ (in $000)	4,830	4,828	4,201	4,164	–
S_{CP} (in $000)	3,804	3,790	3,372	3,400	–
Number of CD transactions	13	11	9	8	15
Number of CP transactions	23	19	14	12	–
Number of RP buys	–	–	–	–	79
Average daily CD + RP interest revenue (in $ per day)	2,646.8	2,613.6	2,461.5	2,414.8	1,247.2
Average daily CP interest cost (in $ per day)	1,399.8	1,391.1	1,217.4	1,216.9	–
Average daily CD and/or RP transaction cost (in $ per day)	3.4	8.7	11.0	13.5	$0.77 \times b$
Average daily profit (in $ per day)	1,243.6	1,213.9	1,233.1	1,184.4	
Firm A's average daily profit (in $ per day)	1,239.5	1,224.1	1,208.7	1,193.4	

5-9 The Four- and Five-asset Symmetric Transaction Cost Model

The firm which has net cash flows with a mean of zero will not always have positive liquid assets. Often it will be in debt. The simple two-asset Miller-Orr model can be "flipped over" to handle this situation. The situation is more complex when one seeks a debt-asset approach analogous to the three-asset Orr model. In this section two alternative models are developed to handle this situation, and the criterion for choosing between the models is outlined.

As outlined in Table 5-7, the extended models assume five-asset accounts:[m] "long" asset balance A, "short" asset balance a, cash balance M, "short" debt balance d, and "long" debt balance D. M_L is assumed to be positive. The firm's net liquid asset balance $T = A + a + M - d - D$. When $T > M_L$, both the four- and the five-asset models are identical to Orr's three-asset model; when $T > M_L$, the status of the models shall be called mode I. Whenever the firm's net liquid asset balance T is less than M_L, the models are operating in mode II.

The models have only three assets active in either mode. In mode I, the "long" asset balance A, the "short" asset balance a, and the cash balance M may be positive, but the "short" debt balance d and the "long" debt balance D are both zero. In mode II, the five-asset model has $A = a = 0$, and M, d, and D are greater than or equal to zero. In mode II, the four-asset model has $A = d = 0$, and M, a, and D are greater than or equal to zero. The four-asset model is so named because the "short" debt balance is always zero.

When the five-asset model is operating under mode II, M is allowed to fluctuate between M_L and $M_L + q$. When one of the limits is violated, enough

Table 5-7
Status Definitions for the Four- and Five-asset Models

	Net Lending Position (Mode I) $A + a + M - d - D \geqslant M_L$		Net Borrowing Position (Mode II) $A + a + M - d - D < M_L$	
Five-asset Model	$A \geqslant 0$ $a \geqslant 0$ $M \geqslant 0$	$d = 0$ $D = 0$	$M \geqslant 0$ $d \geqslant 0$ $D \geqslant 0$	$A = 0$ $a = 0$
Four-asset Model	$A \geqslant 0$ $a \geqslant 0$ $M \geqslant 0$	$d = 0$ $D = 0$	$a \geqslant 0$ $M \geqslant 0$ $D \geqslant 0$	$A = 0$ $d = 0$

---

[m]As in the preceding models, all asset and debt instruments described are those used to manage the liquid asset problem. These models are not concerned with the acquisition of physical assets or projects nor with the issuance of permanent debt.

"short" debt is then issued or retired to return the cash balance to $M_L + r$. When this adjustment in turn forces the "short" debt balance d to violate its control limits 0 or Q, then "long" debt and "short" debt are issued and/or retired to adjust the cash balance to $M_L + r$ and the "short" debt balance to R. The objective function for the expected daily cost of the five-asset model is

$$\min_{\substack{h,z,H,Z \\ q,r,Q,R}} E_5(C) = P(\mathrm{I}) \left[\frac{b_A \sigma^2}{(H-Z)Z} + (i_A - i_a)\frac{H+Z}{3} + \frac{b_a \sigma^2}{(h-z)z} \right.$$

$$\left. + i_A \frac{h+z}{3} + i_A M_L \right] + P(\mathrm{II}) \left[\frac{b_D \sigma^2}{(Q-R)R} \right.$$

$$+ (i_D - i_d)\frac{Q+R}{3} + \frac{b_d \sigma^2}{(q-r)r} + i_D \frac{q+r}{3}$$

$$\left. + i_D M_L \right]$$

where

$P(\mathrm{I})$ = probability of the system being in mode I[n]

$P(\mathrm{II}) = 1 - P(\mathrm{I})$

The first-order conditions give the same values to h, z, H and Z as the three-asset Orr model in Section 5-3. The optimal control limits for mode II are

$$q = 3r \qquad\qquad Q = 3R$$

$$r = \left(\frac{3 b_d \sigma^2}{4 i_D} \right)^{1/3} \qquad R = \left[\frac{3 b_D \sigma^2}{4(i_D - i_d)} \right]^{1/3}$$

---

[n]If $T > M_L$ at the beginning of day 1, then the probability P_n that $T < M_L$ on day n is

$$P_n = \int_{\frac{T-M_L}{\sigma\sqrt{n}}}^{\infty} N_x(m,v)\,dx$$

where

y_i = net cash outflow on day i, generated by $N(0, \sigma^2)$

$l = \sum_{i=1}^{n} y_i$

$m = E(l) = \sum_i \mu_i = 0$

$v = \sum_{i=1}^{n} \sigma_i^2$

$N_x(m,v)$ = the normal distribution on x with mean m and variance v

Then

$$P(\mathrm{II}) = \frac{1}{n} \sum_{i=1}^{n} P_i$$

Substituting the values of the optimal control limits into the expression for the minimum expected daily cost of the five-asset model yields

$$E_{5,\min}(C) = 2P(\text{I}) \left[\left(\frac{3}{4} b_A \sigma^2 \right)^{1/3} (i_A - i_a)^{2/3} \right.$$

$$\left. + \left(\frac{3}{4} b_a \sigma^2 \right)^{1/3} (i_A)^{2/3} \right]$$

$$+ 2P(\text{II}) \left[\left(\frac{3}{4} b_D \sigma^2 \right)^{1/3} (i_D - i_d)^{2/3} \right.$$

$$\left. + \left(\frac{3}{4} b_d \sigma^2 \right)^{1/3} (i_D)^{2/3} \right] + M_L \left[i_A P(\text{I}) + i_D P(\text{II}) \right]$$

When the four-asset model is operating under mode II, M is allowed to fluctuate between its mode II control limits, M_L and $M_L + q$. When one of the limits is violated, then enough "short" assets are sold or purchased to return the cash balance to $M_L = r$. When this adjustment forces the "short" asset balance a to violate its mode II control limits, 0 or Q, then "long" debt is issued or retired to adjust the cash balance to $M_L + r$ and to adjust the "short" asset balance to R. The objective function for the expected daily cost of the four-asset model is

$$\min_{\substack{h, z, H, Z \\ q, r, Q, R}} E_4(C) = P(\text{I}) \left[\frac{b_A \sigma^2}{(H-Z)Z} + (i_A - i_a) \frac{H+Z}{3} + \frac{b_a \sigma^2}{(h-z)z} \right.$$

$$\left. + i_A \frac{h+z}{3} + i_A M_L \right] + P(\text{II}) \left[\frac{b_D \sigma^2}{(Q-R)R} \right.$$

$$\left. + (i_D - i_a) \frac{Q+R}{3} + \frac{b_a \sigma^2}{(q-r)r} + i_D \frac{q+r}{3} + i_D M_L \right]$$

The first-order conditions give the same values to h, z, H, and Z as the three-asset Orr model in Section 5-3. The optimal control limits for mode II in the four-asset model are

$$q = 3r \qquad\qquad Q = 3R$$

$$r = \left(\frac{3 b_a \sigma^2}{4 i_D} \right)^{1/3} \qquad\qquad R = \left[\frac{3 b_D \sigma^2}{4(i_D - i_a)} \right]^{1/3}$$

Substituting the values of the optimal control limits into the expression for the minimum expected daily cost of the four-asset model yields

$$E_{4,\min}(C) = 2P(\text{I}) \left[\left(\frac{3}{4} b_A \sigma^2 \right)^{1/3} (i_A - i_a)^{2/3} \right.$$

$$+ \left(\frac{3}{4} b_a \sigma^2\right)^{1/3} (i_A)^{2/3}\Big]$$

$$+ 2P(\text{II}) \left[\left(\frac{3}{4} b_D \sigma^2\right)^{1/3} (i_D - i_a)^{2/3}\right.$$

$$+ \left(\frac{3}{4} b_a \sigma^2\right)^{1/3} (i_D)^{2/3}\Big]$$

$$+ M_L \Big[i_A P(\text{I}) + i_D P(\text{II})\Big]$$

A comparison between the minimum costs of the four- and five-asset models indicates when one model is preferred.

$$E_{4,\min}(C) - E_{5,\min}(C) = 2P(\text{II}) \left\{\frac{3}{4} b_D \sigma^2 \left[\left(1 - \frac{i_a}{i_D}\right)^{2/3}\right.\right.$$

$$-\left(1 - \frac{i_d}{i_D}\right)^{2/3}\Big]$$

$$+ (i_D)^{2/3} \left(\frac{3}{4}\sigma^2\right)^{1/3} \Big[(b_a)^{1/3} - (b_d)^{1/3}\Big]\Big\}$$

5-10 Questions on the Appropriateness of the Absolute Minimum Cash Balance Constraint

Earlier discussion indicated that the services which a bank offers to a firm are paid for through an arrangement called a "compensating-balance requirement." The firm maintains interest-free deposits which the bank can invest in other areas. The Miller-Orr model and extensions presented in this chapter assume a compensating-balance requirement which specifies an absolute minimum deposit balance which the firm must maintain.

The simulations reported in Tables 5-2, 5-4, and 5-6 show that models with the same absolute minimum balance have markedly different daily revenues and daily profits. The key factor in these differences is not transaction costs but average cash balances. The lower the average cash balance, the higher the profit. Presumably, banks' profit would vary similarly but in the opposite direction.

It is naive to assume that banks value only deposits which they can count on. Yet that is the simple assumption behind the Miller-Orr models. Frost (1970) argues that while banks may value constant deposits above varying deposits, the latter have some positive value. In a dynamic world, the bank of a firm which has reduced its average cash balance might respond to its loss of profits by increasing the absolute minimum deposit constraint under the compensating-balance agreement.

Thus, we must be skeptical of the benefits of the Miller-Orr approach as Orr (1970) applies it to a billion-dollar unnamed corporation. The symmetric transaction cost (h,z) model reduces the number of transactions by more than one-half and brings the mean cash balance from $10.8 million to $2.9 million. The transaction reduction is worth noting, but in fact the cost of these portfolio adjustments over the 18-month period, using the intuitive method and the (h,z) policy, were $1,029 and $483, respectively. This saving is insignificant to most large firms, let alone a billion-dollar giant. The $7.9 million decrease in the mean cash balance is quite impressive, resulting in an increase in interest revenue of over $400,000 annually, but analysis of the supporting data reveals that Orr assumed an absolute minimum cash balance of zero. First, such a low minimum is unrealistic for a firm which must demand sizable check-handling services, lines of credit, and other financial services. Second, if a more appropriate absolute minimum balance had been used and the (h,z) policy still reduced the average cash balance, the bank might either reduce its services to the firm or demand a higher absolute minimum cash balance to cover its loss of profit. Third, if the bank's constraint is actually on the average cash balance, then Orr's analysis is misleading. Since bank profit varies inversely with average cash balance, it seems unreasonable to assume that the bank would allow a $7.9 million decrease in average deposits without drastically reducing services or lines of credit. Hence, the size of the benefits of this modeling effort is still unclear.

Banks may have, in fact, two implicit compensating-balance requirements, but they may specify only the constraint which they feel is binding. The minimum average cash balance constraint determines a lower bound on bank profit. The absolute minimum cash balance protects the bank from covariance of demands for cash among its various firm accounts; for example, firms might all draw down their balances at tax payment time, making it costlier for the bank to lend funds to others at that time.

In conclusion, the models in this chapter were predicated on the absolute minimum balance restriction implicit in the Miller-Orr approach. This restriction allows some of the models to "outperform" Firm A's cash management policy by simply lowering the average cash balance. The resultant increase in interest revenue is the chief reason for this seemingly superior performance. Such performance is misleading, for Firm A's banking constraint requires maintenance of a minimum average cash balance. In Chapter 6 we develop variations on the Miller-Orr approach which are explicitly addressed to the more realistic minimum average cash balance constraint.

Appendix 5A:
Some Characteristics of the Two-asset Cost Function

5A-1 The (h,z) Control Policy

The daily changes in the cash balance are assumed to be generated by a Bernoulli process with a zero mean and a daily variance σ^2. The simple (h,z) control policy allows the cash balance M to fluctuate randomly between a lower bound M_L and an upper bound M_U. Whenever the cash balance violates one of these boundaries, the cash balance is returned to a level $M_L + z$ by purchasing or selling securities. The range over which the cash balance fluctuates is $h = M_U - M_L$.

5A-2 The Expected Daily Transaction Cost of Securities

Miller and Orr (1966) show that in the steady state, the probability $P(T)$ of a forced transfer of assets on a given day (that is, $M \leq M_L$ or $M \geq M_U$ at the end of the day) is

$$P(T) = \frac{\sigma^2}{(h-z)z}$$

$P(T)$ consists of two terms: the probability $P(T_h)$ that M exceeds M_U, and the probability $P(T_0)$ that M is less than M_L at the end of a day.

$$P(T) = P(T_h) + P(T_0)$$

Furthermore,

$$P(T_h) = P(T_h|T)P(T) = \left(\frac{z}{h}\right)P(T) = \frac{\sigma^2}{h(h-z)}$$

$$P(T_0) = P(T_0|T)P(T) = \left(\frac{h-z}{h}\right)P(T) = \frac{\sigma^2}{hz}$$

When transaction costs are lumpy and the cost per transaction of a purchase or of a sale of a security are b_h and b_0, respectively, then the expected daily transaction cost of buying and selling securities is

$$E \text{ (daily transaction cost)} = b_h P(T_h) + b_0 P(T_0)$$

$$= \frac{\sigma^2}{h}\left(\frac{b_h}{h-z} + \frac{b_0}{z}\right)$$

When the costs per transaction are symmetric ($b = b_h = b_o$), then

$$E \text{(daily transaction cost)} = bP(T) = \frac{b\sigma^2}{(h-z)z}$$

5A-3 The Triangular Probability Density Function of Cash; $f_{\widetilde{M}}(M), f_{\widetilde{w}}(w)$

Miller and Orr (1966) show that in the steady state, the probability density function $f_{\widetilde{M}}(M)$ of the cash balance under the (h,z) control policy is triangular. More specifically (see Figure 5A-1), when we define the random variable $M = M_L + \widetilde{w}$, we find

$$f_{\widetilde{w}}(w) = \begin{cases} \dfrac{2}{hz} w & \text{when } 0 < w < z \quad (M_L < M < M_L + z) \\ \dfrac{2}{h(h-z)}(h-w) & \text{when } z < w < h \quad (M_L + z < M < M_U) \\ 0 & \text{elsewhere} \end{cases}$$

$$f_{\widetilde{M}}(M) = f_{\widetilde{w}}(M - M_L)$$

5A-4 The Mean and Variance of a Triangular Density Function; The Expected Daily Opportunity Cost of Holding Cash

$$E(w) = \int_{-\infty}^{\infty} w f_w(w)\, dw = \int_0^z w \frac{2}{hz} w\, dw + \int_z^h w \frac{2}{h(h-z)}(h-w)\, dw$$

$$= \frac{h+z}{3}$$

$$\text{var}(w) = E(w^2) - \left[E(w)\right]^2$$

$$E(w^2) = \int_{-\infty}^{\infty} w^2 f_W(w)\, dw$$

$$= \int_0^z w^2 \frac{2}{hz} w\, dw + \int_z^h w^2 \frac{2}{h(h-z)} (h-w)\, dw$$

$$= \frac{1}{6}\left(h^2 + hz + z^2\right)$$

$$\left[E(w)\right]^2 = \left(\frac{h+z}{3}\right)^2 = \frac{1}{9}\left(h^2 + 2hz + z^2\right)$$

Hence,

$$\text{var}(w) = \frac{1}{18}\left(h^2 - hz + z^2\right)$$

In the Miller-Orr formulation, the expected daily opportunity cost of holding cash equals the product of the (average) daily interest rate i of the highest-yield security available and the expected cash balance $E(M)$.

$$E(M) = \int_{-\infty}^{\infty} M f_{\widetilde{M}}(M)\, dM = M_L + E(w)$$

Hence,

$$E(\text{daily opportunity cost of holding cash}) = M_L i + \frac{h+z}{3} i$$

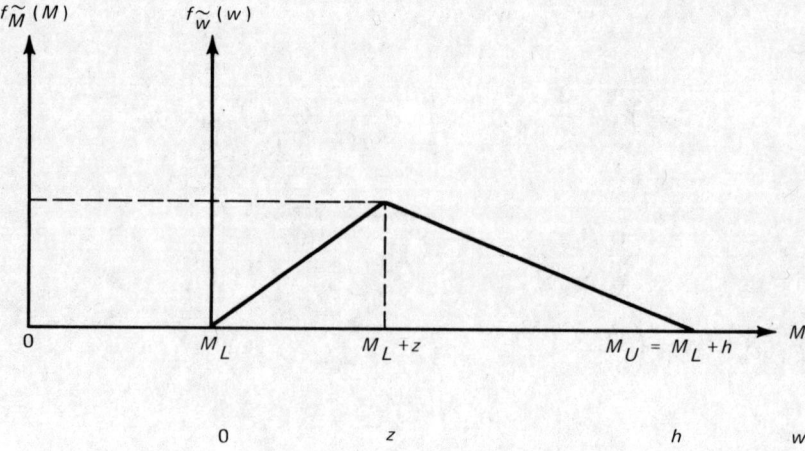

Figure 5A-1. The Probability Density Functions $f_{\widetilde{M}}(M)$ and $f_{\widetilde{w}}(w)$.

Appendix 5B: The Sensitivity of the Two-asset Miller-Orr Minimum Cost, $E(C)$, to Changes in Exogenous Variables

For the two-asset, symmetric transaction cost, absolute minimum cash constraint model:

$$\min_{z,h} E(C) = \frac{b\sigma^2}{(h-z)z} + i\frac{h+z}{3}$$

$$z_{opt} = (3b\sigma^2/4i)^{1/3} \qquad h_{opt} = 3z_{opt}$$

$$E(C)_{min} = \frac{b\sigma^2}{2\left[\frac{3b\sigma^2}{(4i)}\right]^{2/3}} + \frac{4}{3}i\left(\frac{3b\sigma^2}{4i}\right)^{1/3} = (6bi^2\sigma^2)^{1/3}$$

$$\frac{\partial E}{\partial \sigma} = (6bi^2)^{1/3}\left(\frac{2}{3}\sigma^{-1/3}\right) = \frac{2}{3}(6bi^2\sigma^2)^{1/3}/\sigma = \frac{2}{3}E/\sigma$$

$$\frac{\partial E}{\partial b} = (6i^2\sigma^2)^{1/3}\left(\frac{1}{3}b^{-2/3}\right) = \frac{1}{3}\frac{E}{b}$$

$$\frac{\partial E}{\partial i} = (6b\sigma^2)^{1/3}\left(\frac{2}{3}i^{-1/3}\right) = \frac{2}{3}\frac{E}{i}$$

$$dE = \frac{\partial E}{\partial \sigma}d\sigma + \frac{\partial E}{\partial b}db + \frac{\partial E}{\partial i}di$$

$$= \frac{2}{3}E\frac{d\sigma}{\sigma} + \frac{1}{3}E\frac{db}{b} + \frac{2}{3}E\frac{di}{i}$$

$$\frac{dE}{E} = \frac{2}{3}\frac{d\sigma}{\sigma} + \frac{1}{3}\frac{db}{b} + \frac{2}{3}\frac{di}{i}$$

Note that a fractional change of i or σ has twice the impact as the same fractional change of b.

6 Decision Models with a Minimum Average Cash Balance Constraint

6-1 Introduction

In this chapter we deal specifically with the minimum average cash balance constraint. This average is defined over a time period that is mutually acceptable to the firm and its bank. We begin with a discussion of alternative approaches to the minimum average constraint. Then an analytical control limit model is developed which explicitly includes penalty payments for missing the specified average cash balance. Simulation results using these control limits for the last half of Firm A's data are presented for the symmetric transaction cost case. The next section discusses changes in the Miller-Orr model and its variations which adjust the expected cash balance to the target minimum average cash balance. Again, simulation results from these models are reported. The chapter ends with some observations about the success of the various methods of meeting the minimum average cash constraint.

6-2 Approaches to the Minimum Average Cash Balance Constraint

The minimum average cash balance constraint $\bar{M} \geq \bar{M}^*$ can take two general forms; in one case the constraint must be met at any cost, and in the other case a penalty is levied when the constraint is violated. The first form will be called the "rigid" constraint; and the second, the "flexible" constraint.

There are at least two possible ways for a control limit liquid asset decision model to meet the "rigid" minimum average cash balance constraint. The first is to use a Miller-Orr model with fixed control limits over the averaging period, which make the probability of violating the constraint virtually zero. For example, the lower control limit may be set on or above the required minimum average cash balance (that is, $M_L \geq \bar{M}^*$). If the span h of the control limits is greater than zero, this method may lead to unnecessarily high opportunity costs for holding average cash balances which exceed the specified minimum.

A second control limit method for meeting the "rigid" constraint is to build a dynamic programing formulation which recomputes optimal control limits at various time intervals during the averaging period.[a] This approach has the

---
[a]The dynamic programming formulation for the "rigid" constraint was first suggested to the authors by Prof. Robert Merton.

advantage of minimizing opportunity costs by keeping $\bar{M}$ close to $\bar{M}^*$, although the user also must bear the managerial costs of recomputing and adjusting the control limits. Furthermore, unless bounds are placed upon the intermediate control limits, the solution might specify the maintenance of an extremely low cash balance until the last day of the averaging period, whereupon the cash balance must be increased to a phenomenally high level to bring the average balance up to the minimum. Such extreme cash balance behavior might subject the firm's bank to the risk of covariance among client accounts mentioned in Section 5-10, as well as to costly procedures for investing highly variable assets. In such a situation, the implicit absolute minimum cash balance constraint might become binding. Finally, managers may be unwilling to implement changing control limits whose values begin to lose intuitive meaning.[b]

The "relaxed" minimum average cash balance model with penalties for missing the negotiated minimum average contains the ingredients for a contract which enables the firm to pay only for services (and loans) received from its bank in a manner that is administratively simple. Note that the economics of this method do not necessarily dominate the earlier dynamic programming formulation; such dominance depends on the size of penalty, transaction, recomputation, and adjustment costs.[c]

The "relaxed" minimum average cash balance model with penalties is the primary subject for analysis in the remainder of this chapter. The model is developed in the next section.

One should note that the "relaxed" case encompasses the "rigid" case since violation of the rigid constraint can be remedied by borrowing funds. The interest on such borrowing becomes the penalty cost.

6-3 The "Relaxed" Minimum Average Cash Balance Model with Penalties

The development of this model parallels that of the two-asset symmetric transaction cost model in Section 5-2. Of the seven assumptions listed in that section, only the first one is modified for the "relaxed" minimum average model: There is a specified time period called the averaging period, which consists of N_C calendar days and N_B business days. An average cash balance M is computed over the business days N_B.[d] If $\bar{M} \geq \bar{M}^*$, there is no penalty. If $M < M^*$, then the firm is assumed to have borrowed $\bar{M}^* - \bar{M}$ at the bank's loan

---

[b]The dynamic programming approach has been applied by Janssen (1970) to the management of bank reserves for meeting weekly reserve requirements.

[c]Over short averaging periods, the dynamic programming approach would most likely keep $\bar{M}$ closer to $\bar{M}^*$. However, cost considerations not withstanding, implementation of the control rules for the dynamic programming formulation would be far more difficult than for a simple control limit model because of the relative complexity and lack of intuitive appeal of the dynamic programming solution.

interest rate, I_d per N_C-day period. The penalty is the interest payment on the "borrowed" funds [that is, $I_d(\bar{M}^* - \bar{M})$].

The combination of the penalty and opportunity cost functions yields a V-shaped loss curve which is a function of $\bar{M}$. When $\bar{M} > \bar{M}^*$, the firm pays no penalty, but it does incur an opportunity cost of the N_C-day earning asset interest rate I_a for each dollar by which $\bar{M}$ exceeds $\bar{M}^*$. When $\bar{M} < \bar{M}^*$, the firm gains the N_C-day earning asset interest rate but loses the N_C-day borrowing rate for each dollar by which $\bar{M}$ falls short of $\bar{M}^*$; hence, the effective cost per dollar for $\bar{M} < \bar{M}^*$ is $I_d - I_a$. When $\bar{M} = \bar{M}^*$, there is neither a penalty cost nor an opportunity cost. Note that the V-shaped loss curve is not symmetric.

The decision rule for the relaxed minimum average constraint model is simply the same as the two-asset Miller-Orr model. The cash balance M is allowed to fluctuate freely between M_L and M_U (or $M_L + h$). When the control limits are violated, the cash balance is returned to $M_L + z$ through the purchase or sale of earning assets. Since the rules and the stochastic characteristics of the daily net cash inflow are the same, the probability of a transaction and the expected value of the cash balance are the same. That is,

$$P(T) = \frac{\sigma^2}{z(h-z)}$$

$$E(M) = M_L + \frac{h+z}{3}$$

The objective function to be minimized is the expected cost $E_{N_C}(C)$ over the averaging period. This cost consists of the expected transaction cost plus the expected penalty/opportunity cost for having an average cash balance $\bar{M}$. Although the daily cash balances are dependently related to each other, the assumption that each daily cash balance is statistically independent from the others allows the development of a tractable objective function. This assumption becomes more realistic for larger averaging periods. Furthermore, the triangular probability distribution function (developed in Appendix 5A, Section 5A-3) is assumed to adequately represent the distribution of daily cash balances.[e] Hence, the first term of the objective function is simply $N_B b P(T)$ since the probability of N_B independent events is just the sum of the probabilities of each event and since a cost is incurred each time an event takes place. However, the penalty/

---

[d]Although the firm's bank may prefer to average over all N_C days (including weekends and holidays), the average used in this analysis is only over the N_B business days for mathematical and computational convenience.

[e]The assumptions about the triangular probability distribution of the daily cash balances and their stochastic independence are both questionable. Orr (1970) suggests that the steady-state triangular distribution is an adequate representation when $h/\sigma > 6$; this condition is not met for the simulations that follow. The appropriate distribution becomes more peaked around z as h/σ decreases. On the other hand, although the daily cash balances are correlated with each other, their covariance tends to zero as h/σ decreases.

opportunity cost is determined only once, at the end of the averaging period. Given the assumption of statistical independence among the daily cash balances, the appropriate formulation of the probability density function $g(\overline{M})$ which will determine the expected penalty/opportunity cost comes from the *Central Limit theorem*, which states: If the cash balance on any day k is generated by the triangular density function $f(M_k)$ (see Appendix 5A, Section 5A-3) and if

$$\overline{M} = \frac{1}{N_B} \sum_{k=1}^{N_B} M_k$$

then $g(\overline{M})$ is a normal probability density function with mean μ and variance[f] ν where

$$\mu = E(M_k)$$

$$\nu = \frac{1}{N_B} \text{var}(M_k)$$

From Appendix 5A, Section 5A-4,

$$\mu = M_L + \frac{h+z}{3}$$

$$\nu = \frac{h^2 - hz + z^2}{18 N_B}$$

Hence,

$$g(\overline{M}) = \frac{1}{\sqrt{2\pi\nu}} e^{-\frac{1}{2}(\overline{M}-\mu)^2/\nu}$$

Let $C_o = I_d - I_a$ and $C_u = I_a$. The full expression of the objective function to be minimized is

---

[f]The violation of the assumptions (discussed in footnote e) has an impact on the variance ν of $g(\overline{M})$. As h/σ decreases, causing $f(M_k)$ to become more peaked, the variance of $f(M_k)$ [and, therefore, the variance ν of $g(\overline{M})$] decreases. On the other hand, the covariance of the daily cash balances tends to increase ν. However, when the cash balance violates a boundary and returns to $M_L + z$, its future behavior is independent of its history (i.e., it becomes amnesiac). As the number of days in the averaging period increases, the covariance effect on the period variance decreases.

$$\min_{h,z,M_L} E_{N_C}(C) = N_B b P(T) + C_o \int_{-\infty}^{\overline{M}^*} g(x)(\overline{M}^* - x)\, dx + C_u \int_{\overline{M}^*}^{\infty} g(x)(x - \overline{M}^*)\, dx$$

A graphical description of the penalty/opportunity cost loss function is given in Figure 6-1. Needless to say, solving for the first-order conditions of the last equation is hopelessly complex because of the presence of h and z in the argument of the integrals.

It is necessary to solve for h, z, and M_L in stages through the use of approximations and simplifications. First, observe that for a given h and M_L, $P(T)$ is minimized by setting $z = \frac{1}{2} h$. Furthermore, note that the expected penalty/opportunity cost, given h and M_L, is minimized by minimizing v. For a given h, v is minimized by setting $z = \frac{1}{2} h$. Since the components of E_{N_C} are all smallest when $z = \frac{1}{2} h$, this will be the first simplification.

Even with this simplification, the two other first-order conditions cannot be derived easily, principally because the integral expressions are such complex functions of h. Two further simplifications are necessary to solve for h. First, a symmetric triangular function $G(\overline{M})$ is substituted for the normal density function $g(\overline{M})$. $G(\overline{M})$ has the same variance v as $g(\overline{M})$. The second approximation sets the mean of $G(\overline{M})$ at $\overline{M}^*$, not at μ. In reality, the optimal μ should be less than $\overline{M}^*$ because of the asymmetric penalty/opportunity cost loss function. Figure 6-2 displays this simplified version of the loss function. Given these approximations, h can be found by setting

$$\frac{\partial E_{N_C}(C)}{\partial h} = 0$$

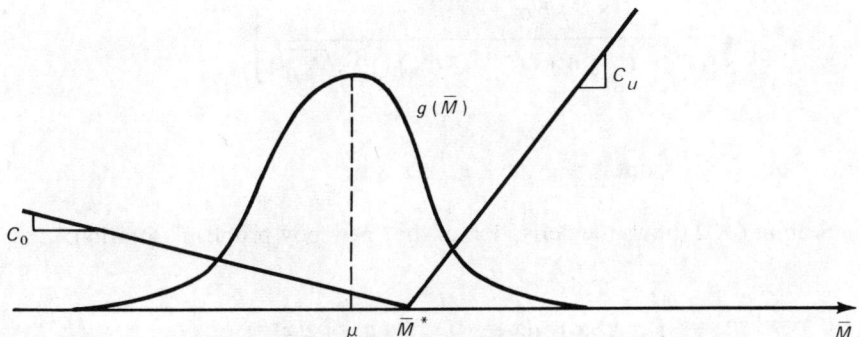

Figure 6-1. The Penalty/Opportunity Cost Loss Function.

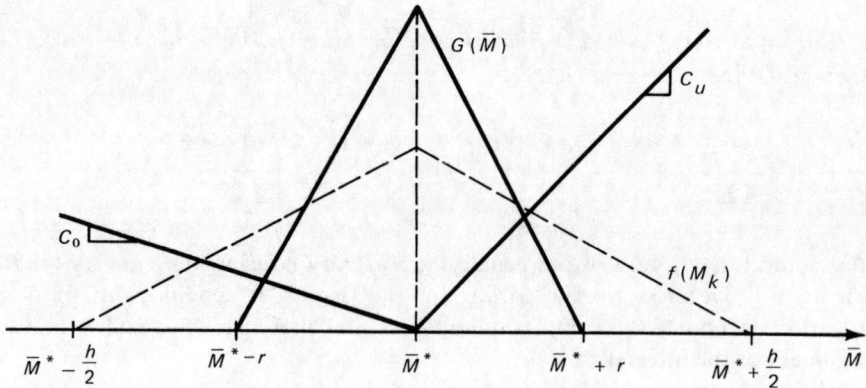

Figure 6-2. Approximation of the Penalty/Opportunity Cost Loss Function.

Once h and z have been approximated, the third stage of the procedure is to use these values in the normal density function $g(\overline{M})$ and solve for an optimal μ (and hence M_L). The method used is commonly called the "newsboy problem."

Recapitulating the three stages in this procedure:

1. Let $z = \frac{1}{2} h$.
2. Approximate the normal $g(\overline{M})$ with the triangular $G(\overline{M})$ where the variance of $G(\overline{M})$ is v and its mean is $\overline{M}^*$. Solve for h.
3. Substitute the values of h and z into normal $g(\overline{M})$ and solve for M_L using the "newsboy problem" approach.

Appendix 6A shows the derivation of h_{opt} in stage 2 of this procedure.

$$h_{opt} = \left[\frac{8 N_B b \sigma^2}{(C_o + C_u)/4 + (C_u - 5 C_o)/(12 \sqrt{N_B})} \right]^{1/3}$$

$$z_{opt} = \frac{1}{2} h_{opt}$$

Section 6A-2 shows the derivation of the "newsboy problem" solution:

$$\frac{C_u}{C_u + C_o} = \int_{-\infty}^{\overline{M}^*} g(x) \, dx = \int_{-\infty}^{\overline{M}^*} N(\mu, v) \, dx$$

where $N(\mu,v)$ is the normal density function with mean μ and variance v. The problem is to find μ given C_0, C_u, $\overline{M}^*$, and v such that the last equation is satisfied. This problem can be solved most easily through the use of the tabulated cumulative of $N(0,1)$ and substitution of variables to convert normal distributions to normalized form.

$$\frac{C_u}{C_u + C_0} = \int_{-\infty}^{\overline{M}^*} N(\mu,v)\, dx = \int_{-\infty}^{y} N(0,1)\, dx$$

where

$$y = \frac{\overline{M}^* - \mu}{\sqrt{v}}$$

That is, one searches the cumulative table of the standardized normal distribution for the y that sets the cumulative to $C_u/(C_u + C_0)$ and then solves for μ:

$$\mu = \overline{M}^* - y\sqrt{v}$$

But

$$\mu = E(M) = M_L + \frac{h+z}{3} = M_L + \frac{h}{2}$$

Hence

$$M_L = \mu - \frac{h}{2}$$

Unfortunately, an analytical expression for M_L in terms of the external variables σ, I_a, I_d, and b is not available, but it can be calculated through the use of normal tables as indicated.

The control limits from the "relaxed" minimum average cash balance model with penalties is applied to a simulation involving data from Firm A. The control limits are calculated using the first 127 business days and are used in a simulation on the next 104 business days, just as in Chapter 5. The 104-business-day period covers 5 months which shall be designated the average period. The interest charge I_a is the cumulative 5-month asset interest and is computed using a yearly rate of 5-7/8%, I_d as the cumulative debt interest and is computed using a yearly rate of 6-7/8%. The minimum average cash balance constraint $\overline{M}^*$ is $3,000,000. Firm A actually had this form of constraint; in Chapter 5, M_L was artificially set to test the modes, but in actuality no absolute minimum cash balance constraint was imposed on the firm. The simulation is executed for symmetric transaction costs $10, $30, $50, and $70. The results are reported in Table 6-1.

This model focuses on $\bar{M}$, the crucial variable in the cash management process. It incorporates the more common banking constraint, the minimum average balance requirement, and targets $\bar{M}$ slightly below the banking constraint ($\bar{M}^*$) while minimizing the variance of $\bar{M}$ subject to transactions and penalty costs. For comparative purposes, profit, revenue, and cost are expressed in daily figures defined over business days, not over calendar days. Note that while opportunity cost was one of the components of the objective function, only real revenue and costs are reported in the table.

Table 6-1
Two-asset Symmetric Transaction Cost Model with Penalty Function on "Relaxed" Average Cash Constraint

	Results of 104-day Simulation Compared with Firm A's Actual Results				
		Two-asset Model			Firm A
b (in $)	10	30	50	70	—
M_L (in $000)	2,587	2,405	2,295	2,211	—
z (in $000)	374	539	640	716	—
h (in $000)	748	1,078	1,280	1,432	—
$\bar{M}$ (in $000)	2,922	2,909	2,920	2,909	3,098
S_M (in $000)	173	232	273	321	642
$\overline{RP}$ (in $000)	—	—	—	—	1,002
S_{RP} (in $000)	—	—	—	—	972
$\overline{CD}$ (in $000)	5,863	5,875	5,864	5,875	4,684
S_{CD} (in $000)	1,683	1,658	1,668	1,660	1,769
Number of CD transactions	38	22	22	20	15
Number of RP buys	—	—	—	—	79
Number of transaction days	38	22	22	20	80
Average daily interest revenue (in $ per day)	1,274.8	1,279.4	1,280.3	1,285.8	1,247.2
Average daily transaction cost (in $ per day)	3.7	6.9	10.6	13.5	$0.77 \times b$
Average daily profit before penalty (in $ per day)	1,271.1	1,272.5	1,269.7	1,272.3	—
Average daily penalty (in $ per day)	21.2	24.5	21.5	24.5	0.0
Average net daily profit (in $ per day)	1,250.0	1,247.9	1,248.2	1,247.9	
Firm A's average daily profit (in $ per day)	1,239.5	1,224.1	1,208.7	1,193.4	

Table 6-1 shows that $\bar{M}$ is lower than $\bar{M}^*$ for each of the b's. In fact, while the actual $\bar{M}$'s increased the interest revenues, the penalty costs associated with the low average balance left the average net daily profit only modestly improved over Firm A's performance.[g]

While an asymmetric transaction cost model should be included in this section for completeness, the analysis is beyond the scope of this book. However, the next section may make such an extension unnecessary. Section 6-4 deals with modifications of the models developed in Chapter 5, making them more appropriate to the minimum average cash balance constraint, rather than to the absolute minimum cash balance constraint. A comparison of the "adjusted" Miller-Orr symmetric transaction cost model with the model presented in this section shows that although the modified Miller-Orr model is conceptually inferior, it produces quite similar results. This suggests that other "adjusted" models from Chapter 5 may produce results similar to the analytically complex extensions of this section.

6-4 Adjusting Miller-Orr Type Models to the Minimum Average Cash Balance Constraint

The modification to the Miller-Orr models of Chapter 5 is quite simple. M_L is set such that

$$\bar{M}^* = E(M) = M_L + \frac{h+z}{3}$$

The values of h and z are not affected by a change in M_L. Note that unlike the model in Section 6-3, there is no attempt to bias $E(M)$ below $\bar{M}^*$ to take advantage of the asymmetric penalty/opportunity cost loss function.

For the "adjusted" symmetric transaction cost Miller-Orr model

$$M_L = \bar{M}^* - \frac{h+z}{3} = \bar{M}^* - \frac{4}{3}z$$

The control limits for this model are determined from the first 127 business days of Firm A's data and are used in a simulation of the last 104 business days. $\bar{M}^*$ equals \$3,000,000. The results of this simulation are reported in Table 6-2. Penalty costs are included in the profit figures.

Note that the average net daily profit from the "adjusted" symmetric transaction cost Miller-Orr model and from the "relaxed" minimum average cash balance model in Section 6-3 are not substantially different. On the average,

---

[g]This comparison between the model and Firm A omits the real-world asymmetric transaction costs.

Table 6-2
"Adjusted" Two-asset Symmetric Transaction Cost Miller-Orr Model with Minimum Average Cash Constraint

		Results of 104-day Simulation Compared with Firm A's Actual Results				
		Two-asset Model				Firm A
b	(in $)	10	30	50	70	–
M_L	(in $000)	2,657	2,505	2,413	2,343	–
z	(in $000)	258	372	440	493	–
h	(in $000)	774	1,116	1,320	1,479	–
$\overline{M}$	(in $000)	2,992	2,975	2,909	2,928	3,098
S_M	(in $000)	170	246	280	342	642
$\overline{RP}$	(in $000)	–	–	–	–	1,002
S_{RP}	(in $000)	–	–	–	–	972
$\overline{CD}$	(in $000)	5,792	5,809	5,875	5,857	4,684
S_{CD}	(in $000)	1,662	1,659	1,709	1,729	1,769
Number of CD transactions		39	30	23	18	15
Number of RP buys		–	–	–	–	79
Number of transaction days		39	30	23	18	80
Average daily interest revenue (in $ per day)		1,260.2	1,267.7	1,281.0	1,277.4	1,247.2
Average daily transaction cost (in $ per day)		3.7	8.7	11.1	12.1	$0.77 \times b$
Average daily profit before penalty (in $ per day)		1,256.4	1,259.1	1,270.0	1,265.3	–
Average daily penalty (in $ per day)		2.1	6.8	24.6	19.6	0
Average net daily profit (in $ per day)		1,254.3	1,252.3	1,245.4	1,245.7	–
Firm A's average daily profit (in $ per day)		1,239.5	1,224.1	1,208.7	1,193.4	

however, one would expect the latter model to show a higher profit than the former because the variance of its $g(\overline{M})$ is less than that of the "adjusted" Miller-Orr model. At the risk of being misled by using only one experiment, it appears that the two models yield similar results.

Simulations of adjusted versions of the two-asset asymmetric transaction cost Miller-Orr model and of the matched loading model are reported in Table 6-3 and Table 6-4, respectively. From the results, it appears clear that the asymmetric transaction cost model performs far better than the matched loading model. While the matched loading model saves approximately $25 per day in

Table 6-3
"Adjusted" Two-asset Asymmetric Transaction Cost Miller-Orr Model with Minimum Average Cash Constraint

		Results of 104-day Simulation Compared with Firm A's Actual Results				
		Two-asset Model				Firm A
b_h	(buy) (in $)	10	30	50	70	—
b_o	(sell) (in $)	767	736	733	740	—
M_L	(in $000)	1,819	1,811	1,796	1,778	—
z	(in $000)	1,514	1,411	1,365	1,340	—
h	(in $000)	2,029	2,159	2,252	2,332	—
$\overline{M}$	(in $000)	2,930	2,857	2,807	2,876	3,098
S_M	(in $000)	476	496	516	616	642
$\overline{RP}$	(in $000)	—	—	—	—	1,002
S_{RP}	(in $000)	—	—	—	—	972
$\overline{CD}$	(in $000)	5,854	5,928	5,977	5,909	4,684
S_{CD}	(in $000)	1,811	1,812	1,824	1,904	1,769
Number of CD transactions		12	12	12	11	15
Number of RP buys		—	—	—	—	79
Number of transaction days		12	12	12	11	80
Average daily interest revenue (in $ per day)		1,269.4	1,289.4	1,295.6	1,282.5	1,247.2
Average daily CD (buy + runoff) + RP transaction cost (in $ per day)		0.8	2.0	3.4	4.0	$0.77 \times b$
Average daily CD sell transaction costs (in $ per day)		29.5	35.4	35.2	35.6	—
Average daily profit before penalty (in $ per day)		1,239.1	1,252.0	1,257.0	1,242.9	—
Average daily penalty (in $ per day)		18.8	38.7	52.1	33.6	0
Average net daily profit (in $ per day)		1,220.3	1,213.3	1,204.9	1,209.3	
Firm A's average daily profit (in $ per day)		1,239.5	1,224.1	1,208.7	1,193.4	

transaction costs, it loses three or four times that amount in reduced net interest revenue, when compared to the asymmetric transaction cost model. Even a narrowing in the difference between the borrowing and lending interest rates may not change this domination.

Another important fact is that Firm A performed almost the same as the asymmetric model and much better than the matched load model. The firm

Table 6-4
"Adjusted" Matched Loading Model with Minimum Average Cash Constraint

Results of 104-day Simulation Compared with Firm A's Actual Results

		Matched Loading Model				Firm A
b	(in $)	10	30	50	70	–
M_L	(in $000)	2,656	2,508	2,426	2,360	–
z	(in $000)	240	360	420	480	–
M_U	(in $000)	3,448	3,624	3,728	3,800	–
$\overline{M}$	(in $000)	3,006	2,973	2,902	2,900	3,098
S_M	(in $000)	182	237	278	321	642
$\overline{RP}$	(in $000)	–	–	–	–	1,002
S_{RP}	(in $000)	–	–	–	–	972
$\overline{CD}$	(in $000)	10,608	10,639	10,083	10,048	4,684
S_{CD}	(in $000)	3,439	3,454	3,001	3,047	1,769
$\overline{CP}$	(in $000)	4,830	4,828	4,201	4,164	–
S_{CP}	(in $000)	3,804	3,790	3,372	3,400	–
Number of CD transactions		13	11	9	8	15
Number of CP transactions		23	19	14	12	–
Number of RP buys		–	–	–	–	79
Average daily CD + RP interest revenue (in $ per day)		2,565.2	2,566.0	2,432.7	2,401.0	1,247.2
Average daily CP interest cost (in $ per day)		1,399.8	1,391.1	1,217.4	1,216.9	–
Average daily transaction cost (in $ per day)		3.4	8.7	11.0	13.5	$0.77 \times b$
Average daily profit before penalty (in $ per day)		1,162.0	1,166.2	1,204.3	1,170.6	–
Average daily penalty (in $ per day)		0.0	7.3	26.5	26.9	0
Average net daily profit (in $ per day)		1,162.0	1,159.0	1,177.8	1,143.7	
Firm A's average daily profit (in $ per day)		1,239.5	1,224.1	1,208.7	1,193.4	

avoided high transaction costs by keeping a buffer balance of RPs, avoided penalty costs by keeping the average cash balance above $\overline{M}^*$, avoided large opportunity costs by keeping $\overline{M}$ close to $\overline{M}^*$ (at least, in the second half of the year), and paid a relatively small opportunity cost for keeping RPs because the difference between the RP and CD rates was smaller than that between the CP and CD rates. On the other hand, Firm A's performance margin drops as the transaction cost involving RP's increases; for b = $70 the adjusted asymmetric model outperforms Firm A. Also, the variance of Firm A's cash balance is much higher than that of the model's. Low variance may result in more banking services or in a lower compensating balance. Furthermore, the use of the simple, routine model should result in savings in managerial time. However, if a firm maintains an average cash balance close to the minimum average required, it is difficult to outperform that firm on purely objective criteria. Interest revenue is the dominant variable.

6-5 Observations on the Minimum Average Cash Constraint Models

The preceding simulations suggest that the "relaxed" minimum average cash balance constraint model and the "adjusted" symmetric transaction cost Miller-Orr model yield similar results. Since the "relaxed" model sets $z = \frac{1}{2} h$ and uses an h that is smaller than that of the "adjusted" Miller-Orr model, the variance of $g(\overline{M})$ is smaller and, on the average, should lead to a greater profit.

All the models in Chapter 6 indicate that while the sizes of the expected transaction and the penalty costs differ widely, their importance compared with interest revenue is relatively small. These costs are usually less than 5% of revenues.

Given the relatively small importance of transaction costs, the essential goal of the liquid-asset manager is to keep the average cash balance as close to the negotiated minimum average as possible.

However, there are two other areas where the models may lead to increased profits. First, if a firm's net cash inflows can be represented by a Gaussian process, then a control limit model can be administered by clerical personnel which would not involve much managerial time and effort. The naive-model approach assures good cash management performance since the probability that the average cash balance will differ significantly from the required average is small. Second, if Frost's contention that banks value the constant portion M_L of a firm's deposits more than the variable portion, then a firm with lower variance in its deposits may be able to negotiate a lower minimum average cash balance agreement. The models display lower variance in deposits than Firm A.

The models discussed in this chapter can provide a simple, systematic approach to good cash management. They focus on the important variable, the average cash balance, but also encompass the impact of transaction cost. Such models allow small and medium-sized firms to routinize the basic cash management process and to allocate managerial time and effort elsewhere.

Appendix 6A: Derivations of the "Relaxed" Minimum Average Cash Balance Model with Penalties

Section 6-3 discusses and gives the results of a three-stage approach to finding the optimum control limits for the "relaxed" minimum average model. Section 6A-1 explains the steps in stage 2. Section 6A-2 explains the steps in stage 3.

6A-1 Analysis of Stage 2

The objective function in its complete form is as follows:

$$\min_{h, z, M_L} E_{N_C}(C) = N_B P(T) + C_0 \int_{-\infty}^{\overline{M}^*} g(x)(\overline{M}^* - x)\, dx$$

$$+ C_u \int_{-\overline{M}^*}^{\infty} g(x)(x - \overline{M}^*)\, dx$$

The stage 2 approximation substitutes triangular distribution $G(\overline{M})$ for normal distribution $g(\overline{M})$. The mean of $G(\overline{M})$ is $\overline{M}^*$, and its variance is v, where

$$v = \frac{1}{18 N_B}\left(h^2 - hz + z^2\right)$$

Since stage 1 assumes $h = \frac{1}{2} z$,

$$v = \frac{h^2}{24 N_B}$$

$G(\overline{M})$ shown graphically in Figure 6-2 has a base equal to $2r$. The variance of this distribution is $r^2/6$. Since this variance must equal v,

$$r = \frac{h}{2\sqrt{N_B}}$$

The expression for $G(\overline{M})$ becomes

$$G(\overline{M}) = \begin{cases} \dfrac{4N_B}{h^2}\left[\overline{M} - \left(\overline{M}^* - \dfrac{h}{2\sqrt{N_B}}\right)\right] \\ \qquad \text{when } \overline{M}^* - \dfrac{h}{2\sqrt{N_B}} < \overline{M} < \overline{M}^* \\ -\dfrac{4N_B}{h^2}\left[\overline{M} - \left(\overline{M}^* + \dfrac{h}{2\sqrt{N_B}}\right)\right] \\ \qquad \text{when } \overline{M}^* < \overline{M} < \overline{M}^* + \dfrac{h}{2\sqrt{N_B}} \\ 0 \qquad \text{elsewhere} \end{cases}$$

The stage 1 and stage 2 assumptions are used in the expression for $E_{N_C}(C)$:

$$E_{N_C}(C) = \dfrac{4N_B b\sigma^2}{h^2} + C_0 \int_A^{\overline{M}^*} (\overline{M}^* - x)\dfrac{4N_B}{h^2}(-A + x)\,dx$$

$$+ C_u \int_{\overline{M}^*}^{D} (x - \overline{M}^*)\dfrac{4N_B}{h^2}(D - x)\,dx$$

where

$$A = \overline{M}^* - \dfrac{h}{2\sqrt{N_B}} \qquad D = \overline{M}^* + \dfrac{h}{2\sqrt{N_B}}$$

Using the well-known integral calculus relation for differentiating an integral, we obtain

$$\dfrac{\partial}{\partial x}\int_{A(x)}^{B(x)} F(x,\xi)\,d\xi = \int_A^B \dfrac{\partial F(x,\xi)}{\partial x}\,d\xi + F(x,B(x))\dfrac{dB}{dx}$$

$$- F(x,A(x))\dfrac{dA}{dx}$$

The first-order condition with respect to h reduces to

$$\frac{\partial E N_B}{\partial h} = \frac{-8 N_B b \sigma^2}{h^3} + C_0 \left(1/4 - \frac{5}{12\sqrt{N_B}}\right) + C_u \left(1/4 + \frac{1}{12\sqrt{N_B}}\right) = 0$$

or

$$h_{opt} = \left[\frac{8 N_B b \sigma^2}{(C_u + C_0)/4 + (C_u - 5C_0)/(12\sqrt{N_B})}\right]^{1/3}$$

For large N_B, the expression simplifies to

$$h_{opt} = \left(\frac{32 b \sigma^2}{I_d / N_B}\right)^{1/3}$$

Note that in the Miller-Orr model

$$h_{opt} = \left(\frac{36 b \sigma^2}{i_a}\right)^{1/3}$$

Hence the solutions have similar form and size.

6A-2 Analysis of Stage 3; the "Newsboy Problem"

This formulation is called the "newsboy problem" because it is traditionally presented as that of a newsboy who faces probability distribution $f(x)$ on the number of newspapers demanded by customers on any given day. If actual demand is above the amount of papers that he has on hand X, he will incur a goodwill cost C_u for each paper demanded above X. If actual demand is below X, he will incur a cost C_0 for each newspaper that he is unable to sell. The newspaper boy is an expected value decisionmaker, and the problem is to choose an X which will minimize his expected cost.

$$E(C) = C_0 \int_0^X (X-x) f(x) \, dx + C_u \int_X^\infty (x-X) f(x) \, dx$$

The first-order condition is found by applying the rule for differentiating an integral, described in Section 6A-1. The first-order condition $dE(C)/dX = 0$ leads to the expression

$$\frac{C_u}{C_u + C_o} = \int_0^X f(x)\,dx$$

That is, one must find an X which satisfies this relationship. If $f(x)$ is a normal distribution, then X must be found through the use of tables.

The stage 3 problem can be converted to a "newsboy problem." The decision problem of stage 3 is to find the M_L which minimizes expected costs, given that h_{opt} and z_{opt} are already known from stage 1 and stage 2. Since the transaction cost term in $E_{N_C}(C)$ depends on h and z but not on M_L, it can be ignored in stage 3. The remaining part of the objective function is

$$C_o \int_{-\infty}^{\overline{M}^*} g(x)(\overline{M}^* - x)\,dx + C_u \int_{\overline{M}^*}^{\infty} g(x)(x - \overline{M}^*)\,dx$$

However, in stage 3, M^* is known but the mean $E(M)$ or μ of $g(x)$ is not known. The "newsboy" solution can be rearranged such that

$$\frac{C_u}{C_o + C_u} = \int_{-\infty}^{\overline{M}^*} g(M, V)\,dx = \int_{-\infty}^{y} N(0,1)\,dx$$

where

$$y = \frac{\overline{M}^* - \mu}{\sqrt{V}} \quad \text{and} \quad \mu = E(M) = M_L + \frac{\overline{h}}{2}$$

The optimal y is found from tables of the standard normal function $N(0,1)$. The optimal M_L is found from the following relation:

$$M_L = \mu - \frac{h_{opt}}{2} = \overline{M}^* - y\sqrt{V} - \frac{h_{opt}}{2}$$

$$= \overline{M}^* - \frac{h_{opt}}{2}\left(1 + \frac{y}{\sqrt{6N_B}}\right)$$

7 A Simulation Approach to Cash Management

The benefits of the Miller-Orr approach are not limited to analytically tractable formulation. In this section a simulation model is developed, based on the concepts underlying the Miller-Orr model. The model is based on two assumptions: the existence of stochastic cash flows, and the appropriateness of the control limit structure. The approach handles the three-asset problem and also the four- and five-asset problems which arise when borrowing becomes necessary. The model allows the decisionmaker to set values for each transaction cost (in and out, for each asset) and for interest rates on the different assets (including falling or rising rates and changes in interest spreads). The decisionmaker determines the maturities of assets and incorporates real-world and policy constraints (e.g., no secondary market for CPs, no discounting of CDs). The manager has several options concerning cash flows. Past cash flows, hypothetical cash flows $[N(0,\sigma^2)]$ generated by the model, predicted hypothetical cash flows, or some combination of these [e.g., some predicted flows in combination with an $N(0,\sigma^2)$ flow] can be used. With a given set of inputs, the model simulates the cash management process and calculates the revenue and cost figures. For a given set of assumptions the manager manipulates the h, z, M_L decision parameters (and H, Z, 0 with three assets, etc.) to maximize net revenue of the cash management process.

The simulation approach does not guarantee optimal results. However, it is flexible enough to include many real-world characteristics of cash management which cannot be incorporated into an analytical approach. It allows the manager's judgments and assumptions to be reflected in the model, and strategies for improving on performance of the simpler Miller-Orr model can be tested. The interaction of the manager and the model in determining the best values for the decision variables (h, z, etc.) gives the manager an intimate knowledge of the nature of the cash management problem.

There are many situations in which this simulation model is able to improve on current techniques and on analytical approaches. The costs of policy constraints can be estimated. The impact of new investment options (e.g., buying higher-return CPs which have no secondary market, instead of treasury bills) can be simulated. One can investigate the impact of changing interest rates and spreads and of different maturity structures. An important situation which can be simulated is the inclusion of deterministic elements in combination with random flows. The effects of being wrong about assumptions (e.g., using a wrong mean or variance of cash flows) can be examined. The approach has the flexibility to reflect a very wide variety of special situations.

For each special situation alternative strategies can be tested, using the model. The manager may try changing maturity structures (fixing maturities to coincide with large predictable flows), choosing certain assets (e.g., investing in RPs overnight to deal with adjacent inflow and outflow days), or employing a heuristic approach which periodically changes h, z control parameters in response to systematic elements in cash flows (see the example below). In conclusion, the model allows the manager to frame the problem, using managerial knowledge and experience to test strategies for dealing with the problem, and to investigate the consequences of being wrong in the assumptions. The model can be implemented with an interactive, time-sharing, graphical display computer device.

A specific example of the use of the simulation model in testing alternative policies in the two-asset case consists of (1) varying the length of maturities purchased, and (2) adjusting the control limits according to which day of the week and to which third of the month the decision is being made. There are several reasons for concern with maturity length. If the length is too short, the firm will be faced with unnecessarily large numbers of runoff and repurchase costs. Furthermore, since the yield curve on debt usually pays higher daily interest for longer maturities, the firm buying very short-term securities may forego the added interest just in case the cash balance does not drop to M_L for a long time. On the other hand, if the length of maturity is too long, it is virtually certain that the firm will be forced to sell the securities before maturity and incur the large sale transaction cost.

Policies concerning day-of-the-week and "week"-of-the-month effects are noteworthy because these effects are observable, partially predictable, and understandable in terms of the payment policy of firms, their customers, and the banking system. There are several ways in which a firm could take advantage of these effects, such as arranging maturity dates to coincide with days exhibiting net cash outflows. However, the approach in this example is to adjust the control limits, so that average daily and weekly effects by themselves will not trigger a transaction. That is, on a given day, h, z, and M_L will be increased (or decreased) by the historical average net cash inflow corresponding to that day of the week and third of the month. The purpose is to lower the amount of transactions associated with managing the liquid assets.

For programing convenience, the different maturity lengths all represent integral weeks. Specifically, the maturity lengths in days are 119, 56, 28, 14, and 7. The day-of-the-week effect T_j and the third-of-the-month effect B_k are calculated from the first 127 business days of Firm A's data. They are

T_1 (Monday)   = −$178,900 B_1 (days 1 to 11) = −$201,600
T_2 (Tuesday)   = $224,800 B_2 (days 12 to 21) = $ 90,500
T_3 (Wednesday)   = −$ 36,800 B_3 (days 22 to 31) = $147,800
T_4 (Thursday)   = $174,200
T_5 (Friday)   = −$157,400

Table 7-1
Summary of Average Daily Profits (in $000) after Penalty Cost under Different Policies with the Symmetric Miller-Orr Model with Absolute Minimum Constraint

Length of Maturity (days)	Cost per Transaction, b ($)			
	10	30	50	70
119	1.3363[a]	1.3049	1.2952	1.2750
	1.3376[b]	1.3034	1.2945	1.2782
	1.3436[c]	1.3083	1.2844	1.2704
56	1.2743	1.2413	1.2253	1.2043
	1.2708	1.2406	1.2337	1.2170
	1.2775	1.2357	1.2130	1.1995
28	1.2332	1.2001	1.1841	1.1613
	1.2325	1.2007	1.1901	1.1591
	1.2352	1.2021	1.1779	1.1505
14	1.2250	1.1919	1.1644	1.1342
	1.2275	1.1842	1.1716	1.1450
	1.2255	1.1900	1.1656	1.1345
7	1.2035	1.1762	1.1534	1.1190
	1.2153	1.1815	1.1564	1.1377
	1.2172	1.1830	1.1492	1.1294

[a]First element in each cell results from policies ignoring systematic effects.
[b]Second element in each cell results from policies taking account of the day-of-the-week systematic effect.
[c]Third element in each cell results from policies taking account of both the day-of-the-week systematic effect and the third-of-the-month effect.

Table 7-2
Summary of Average Daily Profits (in $000) after Penalty Cost under Different Policies with the Asymmetric Miller-Orr Model with Absolute Minimum Constraint

	Costs per Transaction: b_o, b_n ($)			
Length of Maturity (days)	10 767	30 736	50 733	70 740
119	1.1312[a] 1.1348[b] 1.0919[c]	1.1425 1.1533 1.1124	1.1441 1.1495 1.1127	1.1259 1.1528 1.1145
56	1.0592 1.0637 1.0302	1.0725 1.0885 1.0478	1.0803 1.0805 1.0504	1.0772 1.0835 1.0536
28	1.0308 1.0294 0.9941	1.0374 1.0456 0.9936	1.0424 1.0492 0.9964	1.0371 1.0511 0.9980
14	1.005 1.0114 0.9995	1.0024 1.0158 1.0012	1.0013 1.0192 1.0057	0.9935 1.0187 1.0050
7	0.9630 0.9742 0.9782	0.9543 0.9874 0.9877	0.9554 0.9691 0.9703	0.9539 0.9663 0.9682

[a]First element in each cell results from policies ignoring systematic effects.
[b]Second element in each cell results from policies taking account of the day-of-the-week systematic effect.
[c]Third element in each cell results from policies taking account of both the day-of-the-week systematic effect and the third-of-the-month effect.

Table 7-3
Summary of Average Daily Profits (in $000) after Penalty Cost under Different Policies with the Matched Load Miller-Orr Model with Absolute Minimum Constraint

Length of Maturity (days)	Cost per Transaction, b ($)			
	10	30	50	70
119	1.2436[a]	1.2139	1.2331	1.1844
	1.2440[b]	1.2189	1.2319	1.2144
	1.2379[c]	1.2136	1.2005	1.1811
56	1.2022	1.1805	1.1729	1.1492
	1.1952	1.1778	1.1799	1.1666
	1.1935	1.1693	1.1489	1.1491
28	1.1848	1.1624	1.1477	1.1228
	1.1789	1.1567	1.1525	1.1394
	1.1843	1.1570	1.1415	1.1317
14	1.1906	1.1675	1.1448	1.1235
	1.1895	1.1634	1.1500	1.1363
	1.1928	1.1603	1.1441	1.1297
7	1.1970	1.1710	1.1493	1.1251
	1.1943	1.1670	1.1515	1.1326
	1.1981	1.1652	1.1512	1.1323

[a] First element in each cell results from policies ignoring systematic effects.
[b] Second element in each cell results from policies taking account of the day-of-the-week systematic effect.
[c] Third element in each cell results from policies taking account of both the day-of-the-week systematic effect and the third-of-the-month effect.

Table 7-4
Summary of Average Daily Profits (in $000) after Penalty Cost under Different Policies with the Symmetric Model with Penalty and Relaxed Average Constraint

Length of Maturity (days)	Cost per Transaction, b ($)			
	10	30	50	70
119	1.2500[a]	1.2479	1.2482	1.2479
	1.2557[b]	1.2469	1.2427	1.2406
	1.2571[c]	1.2490	1.2479	1.2380
56	1.1913	1.1922	1.1911	1.1809
	1.1943	1.1847	1.1795	1.1800
	1.1941	1.1836	1.1784	1.1715
28	1.1617	1.1554	1.1510	1.1410
	1.1561	1.1461	1.1404	1.1413
	1.1570	1.1464	1.1388	1.1342
14	1.1440	1.1395	1.1311	1.1238
	1.1467	1.1416	1.1320	1.1245
	1.1512	1.1433	1.1305	1.1226
7	1.1279	1.1132	1.1043	1.1916
	1.1315	1.1185	1.1086	1.1035
	1.1327	1.1186	1.1054	1.0972

[a]First element in each cell results from policies ignoring systematic effects.

[b]Second element in each cell results from policies taking account of the day-of-the-week systematic effect.

[c]Third element in each cell results from policies taking account of both the day-of-the-week systematic effect and the third-of-the-month effect.

Table 7-5
Summary of Average Daily Profits (in $000) after Penalty Cost under Different Policies with the Symmetric Miller-Orr Model with Minimum Average Constraint

Length of Maturity (days)	Cost per Transaction, b ($)			
	10	30	50	70
119	1.2543[a]	1.2523	1.2457	1.2457
	1.2577[b]	1.2480	1.2434	1.2378
	1.2562[c]	1.2456	1.2417	1.2414
56	1.1959	1.1920	1.1856	1.1854
	1.1969	1.1869	1.1810	1.1757
	1.1940	1.1826	1.1824	1.1825
28	1.1576	1.1521	1.1455	1.1408
	1.1582	1.1471	1.1388	1.1286
	1.1566	1.1431	1.1414	1.1333
14	1.1476	1.1382	1.1345	1.1256
	1.1465	1.1393	1.1305	1.1177
	1.1506	1.1360	1.1290	1.1149
7	1.1239	1.1184	1.1065	1.0887
	1.1307	1.1166	1.1000	1.0894
	1.1320	1.1172	1.0976	1.0859

[a]First element in each cell results from policies ignoring systematic effects.

[b]Second element in each cell results from policies taking account of the day-of-the-week systematic effect.

[c]Third element in each cell results from policies taking account of both the day-of-the-week systematic effect and the third-of-the-month effect.

Table 7-6
Summary of Average Daily Profits (in $000) after Penalty Cost under Different Policies with the Asymmetric Miller-Orr Model with Minimum Average Constraint

Length of Maturity (days)	Cost per Transaction: b_o, b_h ($)			
	10 767	30 736	50 733	70 740
119	1.2203[a]	1.2133	1.2049	1.2093
	1.2089[b]	1.2066	1.1975	1.1966
	1.1998[c]	1.2947	1.1978	1.1937
56	1.1591	1.1577	1.1523	1.1489
	1.1588	1.1527	1.1427	1.1376
	1.1302	1.1439	1.1451	1.1402
28	1.1259	1.1348	1.1299	1.1278
	1.1260	1.1278	1.1232	1.1168
	1.0907	1.0958	1.0976	1.1029
14	1.0972	1.1045	1.0977	1.0952
	1.1048	1.1155	1.1219	1.1159
	1.0968	1.1130	1.1063	1.1088
7	1.0597	1.0534	1.0498	1.0517
	1.0678	1.9835	1.0682	1.9690
	1.0729	1.0838	1.0694	1.0708

[a] First element in each cell results from policies ignoring systematic effects.
[b] Second element in each cell results from policies taking account of the day-of-the-week systematic effect.
[c] Third element in each cell results from policies taking account of both the day-of-the-week systematic effect and the third-of-the-month effect.

Table 7-7
Summary of Average Daily Profits (in $000) after Penalty Cost under Different Policies with the Matched Load Miller-Orr Model with Minimum Average Constraint

Length of Maturity (days)	Cost per Transaction, b ($)			
	10	30	50	70
119	1.1620[a]	1.1590	1.1778	1.1437
	1.1583[b]	1.1631	1.1729	1.1711
	1.1439[c]	1.1467	1.1552	1.1459
56	1.1265	1.1281	1.1330	1.1268
	1.1199	1.1226	1.1269	1.1201
	1.1104	1.1044	1.1060	1.1158
28	1.1118	1.1124	1.1086	1.9997
	1.1066	1.1037	1.1007	1.0937
	1.1043	1.9941	1.1029	1.1025
14	1.1172	1.1123	1.1101	1.1027
	1.1151	1.1065	1.1028	1.0949
	1.1122	1.1046	1.1051	1.0965
7	1.1189	1.1134	1.1069	1.1000
	1.1184	1.1085	1.1007	1.0899
	1.1182	1.1089	1.1020	1.0913

[a]First element in each cell results from policies ignoring systematic effects.

[b]Second element in each cell results from policies taking account of the day-of-the-week systematic effect.

[c]Third element in each cell results from policies taking account of both the day-of-the-week systematic effect and the third-of-the-month effect.

Tables 7-1 through 7-7 display the simulated daily profit after transaction cost and after penalty payments for three models developed in Chapter 5 and for four models developed in Chapter 6. The simulation uses the second half of Firm A's data as its input. Each profit "triplet" in the tables for a given cost per transaction and for a given maturity length represents a different policy. The first element is the profit result when neither the day-of-the-week nor the third-of-the-month effects are considered. The second element is generated from a control limit model that is adjusted for only the day-of-the-week effects (T's). The third profit figure is the result of adjusting the control limits for both the day-of-the-week effect (T's) and the third-of-the-month effect (B's).

The tables show quite clearly that the length of maturity is a significant factor in the profit performance and that with a slight exception in Table 7-3, all the models perform better as the maturity length is increased. The policies adjusting the control limits to the systematic day-of-the-week and third-of-the-month effects do not show any consistent performance improvement over policies which ignore these effects.

As stated earlier, the purpose of shifting the control limits in accordance with the systematic effects in those data is to avoid transaction costs, especially the large costs of selling a security. The inability of these policies to effect systematic improvements in profit performance reaffirms that the key to profit is the average cash balance rather than transaction costs.

Of course, other experiments may be performed with the simulation model. One obvious candidate would be setting maturities of securities so that runoff occurs on days for which the manager forecasts a net cash outflow. The analytical models described earlier do not allow such flexibility. This model allows the manager to test many heuristic approaches to improve cash management.

8 Forecasting in Cash Management

This chapter is essentially a digression from the central focus of this study. In it we discuss several issues concerning Firm A's current method of cash management and the effects of attempts to forecast cash flows.

Earlier we alluded to the "sharp pencil" approach to cash management. The objective of this approach is to minimize the total assets committed to cash management. Financial resources are considered scarce and expensive. Financial resources squeezed out of cash management can be used to finance profitable projects which await funding. Hence, the holding of earning assets as well as cash results in an opportunity cost. Therefore, the firm seeks to minimize the variance of the cash balance while keeping the average cash balance at the minimum required compensating average. Reducing the variance of cash frees "idle" earning assets for other uses and reduces interest charges from borrowing. Lower variance may also allow the firm to negotiate increased banking services and/or a reduction in compensating-balance requirement and reduce the difficulty in achieving the required average cash balance. Hence, the approach tries to keep the cash balance close to the required average, thereby reaping the benefits of a reduced variance of cash balance and satisfying banking constraints. Transaction costs are considered negligible in comparison with the benefits of keeping a low cash balance. Often forecasting of cash flows plays an important role in the control of cash balances. Following Orr (1970), the firm's decision rule is of the form

$$C_t = \alpha(M_t^* - M_{t-1}) - \hat{F}_t \qquad 0 < \alpha \leq 1 \qquad (8.1)$$

where C_t is the control action (purchase or sale of earning asset), α the adjustment smoothing coefficient, $\hat{F}_t$ is the forecast of net cash flow for period t, M_{t-1} is the cash balance at the end of period $t-1$ and M_t^* is the target cash balance for period t (i.e., the compensating balance). The cash balance changes accordingly:

$$M_t = M_{t-1} + C_t + F_t \qquad (8.2)$$

where F_t is the actual net cash flow in period t. This linear adjustment approach is appropriate as long as there is no significant or large lumpy cost to transactions. The rationale behind this approach conforms well with the description of Firm A's cash management procedures. They consider transaction cost negligible, and to a certain extent, they forecast cash flows by using their knowledge and experience. Their objective in daily control actions is to keep balances near the compensating balance. With this framework we will briefly examine their forecasting and control performance.

Harlan D. Mills (1967) showed that there are constraints on a firm's ability to reduce the variability in cash balances when cash flows have a fundamental variability. There is a smoothing frontier, and no control policy can reduce variability below this frontier unless there is specific information about cash flows. The frontier is

$$\frac{\sigma_M}{\sigma_F} \geqslant \frac{1}{2} \left(\frac{\sigma_C}{\sigma_F} + \frac{\sigma_F}{\sigma_C} \right)$$

In the case of Firm A,

$$1.44 \geqslant 1.06$$

We can evaluate control policies against this criterion. If a policy yields ratios above the frontier, then the policy is increasing the variability in the system.[a] This is acceptable if it is in response to lumpy transaction costs. In that case, the larger variability in cash balances yields a reduction in transaction costs. If transaction costs are considered negligible, then a control policy which yields results beyond the frontier is actually hurting cash management performance in the "sharp pencil" framework. This might often be the case with the "sharp pencil" approaches designed to minimize cash balances which actually result in increased variability of cash balance. The smoothing frontier is not difficult to achieve, however. Using the expected value of cash flows as one's daily forecast yields results on the minimum variance smoothing frontier. Bad performance is the result of poor forecasting and inappropriate control actions on days when no forecast is made.

Hence, a firm has two choices. It can reduce variance to the level of the "smoothing frontier" by using the naive forecast (i.e., expected value of daily cash flows), or it can attempt to achieve performance within the frontier by using forecast information. In the latter case, forecasting, the firm incurs risks of counterproductive results. First, the variance may be increased because the firm is not incorporating good forecasts into control action in a systematic way [such as the linear adjustment rule, Equation (8.1)]. Second, the firm may be making poor forecasts. Third, the firm may make good forecasts on certain days and incorporate them systematically in a control policy, but may have an inappropriate policy for control actions on days on which no confident forecast can be made. This can increase the variance of the cash balances. Finally, the benefits from good forecasting may be outweighed by its cost.

---

[a]See Harlan D. Mills. "Smoothing in Inventory Processes," in Shubik (ed.). *Essays in Mathematical Economics in Honor of Oskar Morgenstern.* Princeton: Princeton University Press, 1967. See also Daniel Orr. *Cash Management and the Demand for Money.* New York: Praeger Publishers, 1970, pp. 152-158.

The performance of Firm A's control policy was indicated earlier. The firm is operating reasonably close to the smoothing frontier. However, its policy is inferior to the naive approach of using the expected value of cash flows as forecasts. If we assume Firm A is implicitly using a control policy of the form of Equation (8.1), then we can calculate the correlations of the forecasts and cash flows implicit in their control policy for given α's. This approach is tenuous, but their description of their control policy coincides well with the assumptions underlying Equation (8.1). Similarly, the world cannot distinguish between explicit forecasts and implicit forecasts arising from a policy. Hence, in terms of cash management performance, we cannot distinguish between a calculated forecast by the firm on a given day and an uninformed action (or inaction) on a no-forecast day, which yields an implicit forecast ($\hat{F}$) which is not optimal (i.e., not equal to the expected value of net cash flows). For a policy to work well, on every day for which no forecast is available $\hat{F}$ should be equal to the expected value of cash flows (zero in Firm A's case). Poor performance is the result of poor forecasts and inappropriate action on days for which there is no forecast. A firm's gains in terms of reduced variance from expertise in forecasting can be offset by the lack of a systematic, optimal policy of control actions on days for which no forecast can be made. Table 8-1 displays the correlation of Firm A's forecasts with cash flows. If we assume $\alpha = 1$, the criterion for forecasting control reduces to

$$\sigma_{\hat{F}} \geqslant 2\rho\sigma_F$$

Their forecasting harms operating performance if this inequality holds. In our case,

$$802 > 512$$

Hence, forecasting harms performances (i.e., increases variance of cash balance) because correlation of forecasts and cash flow is too small and because variance of the forecasts is too large. It is clear that Firm A may have some accurate information on which to base forecasts for certain days. Their difficulties could arise from an inability to incorporate good forecasts systematically into their control policy and inappropriate handling of days on which no good forecast can be made.

This analysis outlines some dangers from poor forecasting and poorly designed control policies when stochastic cash flows are present. If a firm believes lumpy transaction costs are not important, it should investigate linear adjustment policies such as the one described in this section. Because our study is predicated on the handling of lumpy transaction costs, we do not pursue this line of investigation.

A specific problem implicit in this analysis is the difficulty of incorporating

Table 8-1
Firm A's Implicit Forecasts (Deduced by Applying Decision Rule (1) to data)

α	r	$S_{\hat{F}}$
0.1	0.491	662.4
0.3	0.523	606.6
0.5	0.518	635.6
0.7	0.485	704.1
0.9	0.441	801.8

α = assumed speed-of-adjustment parameter in linear adjustment decision rule (1).
r = resulting sample correlation coefficient of hypothetical daily forecasts and net daily cash flows.
$S_{\hat{F}}$ = sample standard deviation of hypothetical daily forecasts.

good forecasts in a cash management control policy. The problem can be attacked heuristically, employing the simulation model described in Chapter 7. Future research might focus on analytic formulations of the problem. The maturity selection problem can be included in such a formulation. Inflows at maturity can be considered large flows which can be forecasted. The firm has some discretion over the timing of maturity flows, as well as over other large predictable flows (e.g., dividends, etc.). The analytical approach would seek to develop an optimal control policy for cash flows consisting of discretionary, predictable flows mixed with the stochastic flows. This is an area for future research.

It should be clear from the previous chapters that any forecasting approach must prove its usefulness against a Miller-Orr naive benchmark. A more complex and costly forecasting approach must demonstrate incremental benefits when compared with the efficacy, simplicity, and low cost of the Miller-Orr approach.

9 Conclusion

This book has focused on approaches to cash management. Naive decision models have been developed and evaluated with data from a medium-sized unnamed firm. Clearly, the analysis of the statistical nature of Firm A's net cash flows adds another chapter of empirical support to the case for naive decision models. The major statistical assumptions underlying the original Miller-Orr model and its extensions are confirmed by our analysis of net cash flows of Firm A. These cash flows were found to be normally distributed with a mean of zero. This distribution was found to be stable over time. Statistically significant daily and weekly systematic effects were detected, and the appropriate selection of maturity dates in conjunction with a naive model might improve performance.

The other assumptions of the Miller-Orr model were generally supported in the case of Firm A. One notable exception was Firm A's banking constraint which requires a minimum average balance rather than the absolute minimum balance. Another exception concerns Firm A's policy of investing in two earning assets rather than one, as the Miller-Orr model assumes. Firm A's two-asset policy is designed to avoid the high transfer cost involved in selling CDs. Thus, the assumption of symmetry of transaction cost is also violated.

These exceptions account for the apparently superior performance of the basic Miller-Orr model when applied to the data. This performance is due to the model's low average cash balance and the ignoring of the high transaction cost involved in discounting earning assets. Two models were developed to incorporate the latter aspect of the cash management problem. The asymmetric transaction cost model and the matched loading model are able to handle this characteristic of the business environment within the general framework of the Miller-Orr approach. The Miller-Orr approach was also extended in the development of the four- and five-asset models. These models routinize the cash management process during periods of negative as well as positive liquid assets. However, this entire class of model assumes an absolute minimum compensating-balance requirement. Their results are inappropriate and misleading if the banking constraint is a minimum average balance requirement. This issue is critical, since the average cash balance determines interest revenue, a key factor in cash management profitability.

All this leads to a major contention of this book. Just as the average cash balance is important in determining a firm's cash management performance, it is also the critical variable in banking profitability. Hence, as in the case of Firm A, compensating-balance constraints can be expected to focus on the average balance, as opposed to the absolute minimum balance constraint inherent in the Miller-Orr approach. For models to be useful to management they must focus on the average balance and incorporate a banking constraint on the average balance. The model developed in Chapter 6 is preferable to the Miller-Orr approach because it is motivated by these considerations. It is designed to position the average cash balance subject to the penalty and opportunity costs involved in missing the compensating-balance constraint, and it also includes the effects of lumpy transaction costs. This model is also superior to the Miller-Orr approach because the return point (z) is in the center of the control range ($\frac{1}{2} h$) rather than off center ($z = \frac{1}{3} h$, in Miller-Orr). Thus the variance of the average cash balance is reduced, resulting in lower opportunity and penalty costs in the long run as well as lower transaction costs. Although this model is conceptually superior to the adjusted Miller-Orr model discussed in Chapter 6, the absolute magnitude of its comparative benefits may be small. The adjusted Miller-Orr approach has the advantage of its simplicity, and its amenability to modification to include more complex real-world considerations (e.g., asymmetric transaction costs).

These latter models are the only ones really relevant in testing against Firm A's performance. They do not improve significantly upon the profitability of Firm A's cash management. The policy of having a buffer of RPs allows Firm A to avoid discounting CDs. Although it results in a large number of transactions, transaction costs are relatively insignificant in cash management profitability. However, the key to Firm A's success at cash management is its ability to keep the average cash balance close to the required average over the test period. Since this results in near maximum interest revenue, it is difficult for any model to improve significantly upon this performance.

This does not mean that such models are not useful. Several specific advantages of these models have been discussed. These advantages have greatest appeal to small and to medium-sized firms. In general, they provide simple, systematic decision rules which ensure profitable cash management with a minimum of managerial time and effort. They ensure an average cash balance close to the required average, resulting in high interest revenue. Hence, it is very difficult to improve upon the performance of such naive models. Even if cash flows could be forecasted effectively and if managerial time and effort were allocated to this task, the potential gains would be small. Transaction cost gains are relatively insignificant, and as long as the naive approach yields average cash balances close to the required average, alternative methods cannot significantly improve upon it. Once the basic cash management process has been routinized, the simulation model described in Chapter 7 can be used to investigate new earning asset or loan instruments, strategies for handling extraordinary periods in the cash flow process, and a wide variety of other special situations.

As favorable empirical evidence accumulates and as the models described herein become accepted, future research may focus on incorporating discretionary, predictable large cash flows into the basic analytical framework of these models. The statistical analysis in Chapter 4 suggests this approach; there seem to be two distinct distributions of net cash flows, one of large systematic (perhaps predictable) flows, the other a normal distribution of smaller cash flows. Such large predictable cash flows as tax and dividend payments would be included. Maturity determination could be included in such a framework, for the maturity of an earning asset can be considered as a predictable, discretionary large cash flow. Such a model would further routinize the cash management process, freeing managerial resources for other tasks.

Another important area of future research is suggested in the discussion of the compensating balance in this book. The real net cost of the minimum average compensating-balance constraint is the difference between the opportunity cost of holding the average compensating balance above the average transactions demand balance (necessary for the firm's operation) and the value of the bank's services to the firm. Furthermore, an average compensating-balance constraint allows the firm to let its cash balance wander freely throughout most of the averaging period. Very few strategic transactions are required to satisfy the average balance requirement. Hence, the average compensating-balance constraint allows the firm to reduce its transaction costs. These transactions which the firm now avoids can be carried out more cheaply by banks. Banks have the advantage of the pooling effects of changes in many firms' cash balances (i.e., some of these changes are offsetting). Furthermore, banks have expertise and economies of scale in the business of making transactions. Banks have the additional advantage of access to the federal funds market, which gives them flexibility and efficiency in making transactions that small and medium-sized firms cannot match. Banks may be compensated for their intermediation in this case by slightly higher interest rates on lines of credit to firms. These advantages provide a rationale for the existence of compensating balances as a device allowing banks to carry out money-market operations for firms. This rationale is also consistent with the absence of well-developed markets in commercial paper for small and medium-sized firms. Banks can handle transactions more cheaply than such markets, and compensating-balance arrangements allow them to perform these tasks for firms. This rationale is empirically testable and is an area for future research.

For economists, perhaps the most important area of future research concerns the implication of this work for the demand for money and other major economic variables. As Miller and Orr point out, these models introduce the variance of cash flows as an important variable. Our work implies that economists should not focus exclusively on firms' demand for money. It underlines the importance of compensating-balance restrictions set by banking institutions and suggests research into the setting of such constraints and into the sensitivity of these constraints to changes of important economic variables such as interest rates.

In conclusion, the modeling of the cash management process provides not only useful, practical decision rules for business managers, but also fruitful input to monetary economics.

Bibliography

Bibliography

Baumol, William J. "The Transactions Demand for Cash: An Inventory Theoretic Approach." *Quarterly Journal of Economics*, Vol. 66, 1952, pp. 545-556.

Eppen, Gary D., and Fama, Eugene F. "Solutions for Cash Balance and Simple Dynamic Portfolio Problems." *Journal of Business*, Vol. 41, 1968, pp. 94-112.

Eppen, Gary D., and Fama, Eugene F. "Cash Balance and Simple Dynamic Portfolio Problems with Proportional Costs." *International Economic Review*, Vol. 10, June 1969, pp. 119-133.

Eppen, Gary D., and Fama, Eugene F. "Three Asset Cash Balance and Dynamic Portfolio Problems." *Management Science*, Vol. 17, January 1971, pp. 311-319.

Feller, William. *An Introduction to Probability Theory and Its Applications.* Vol. 1. New York: John Wiley & Sons, Inc. 1951.

Freeman, Harold. *Introduction to Statistical Inference.* Reading, Mass.: Addison-Wesley Publishing Company, Inc. 1963.

Frost, Peter. "Banking Services, Minimum Cash Balances, and the Firm's Demand for Money." *Journal of Finance*, Vol. 25, 1970, pp. 1029-1039.

Gibson, William E. "Compensating Balance Requirements." *National Banking Review*, March 1965, pp. 387-395.

Girgis, Nadia M. "Optimal Cash Balance Levels." *Management Science*, November 1968, pp. 130-140.

Hausman, Warren. "The Stochastic Cash Balance Problem with Average Compensating Balance Requirements." Working paper, Sloan School of Management, M.I.T., January 1973.

Homonoff, Richard B., and Mullins, David W. *Cash Management: Applications and Extensions of the Miller-Orr Control Limit Approach.* Master's Thesis, Sloan School of Management, M.I.T., 1972.

Janssen, Christian T.L. *An Information-decision System for Bank Reserve Management; A Dynamic Programming Decision Model Based upon Exponentially Smoothed Forecasts of Interest Rates.* Unpublished doctoral dissertation, Cornell University, 1970.

Keynes, John M. *The General Theory of Employment, Interest and Money.* New York: Harcourt Brace Jovanovich, Inc. 1936.

Miller, Merton H., and Orr, Daniel. "A Model of the Demand for Money by Firms." *Quarterly Journal of Economics*, Vol. 80, 1966, pp. 413-435.

Miller, Merton H., and Orr, Daniel. "An Application of Control Limit Models to the Management of Corporate Cash Balances," in Robichek (ed.). *Financial Research and Management Decisions.* New York: John Wiley & Sons, Inc. 1967.

Miller, Merton H., and Orr, Daniel. "The Demand for Money by Firms: Extensions of Analytic Results." *Journal of Finance*, Vol. 23, 1968, pp. 735-759.

Mills, Harlan D. "Smoothing in Inventory Processes," in Shubik (ed.). *Essays in Mathematical Economics in Honor of Oskar Morgenstern*. Princeton: Princeton University Press. 1967.

Neave, Edwin H. "The Stochastic Cash Balance Problem with Fixed Costs for Increases and Decreases." *Management Science*, Vol. 16, March 1970, pp. 472-490.

Orgler, Yair E. "An Unequal-period Model for Cash Management Decisions." *Management Science*, Vol. 16, October 1969, pp. 77-92.

Orr, Daniel. *Cash Management and the Demand for Money*. New York: Frederick A. Praeger, Inc. 1970.

Porteus, Evan L., and Neave, Edwin H. "The Stochastic Cash Balance Problem with Charges Levied against the Balance." *Management Science*, Vol. 18, July 1972, pp. 600-602.

Porteus, Evan L. "Equivalent Formulations of the Stochastic Cash Balance Problem." *Management Science*, November 1972, pp. 250-253.

Siegel, Sidney. *Nonparametric Statistics*. New York: McGraw-Hill Book Company. 1956.

Weitzman, Martin. "A Model of the Demand for Money by Firms: Comment." *Quarterly Journal of Economics*, Vol. 82, 1968, pp. 161-164.

Index

Adjusted Miller-Orr models, 69-73
Analysis of variance, 20, 21, 23
Asymmetric transaction cost models, 43-49, 69-73, 82, 83, 86-88

Banking services, 38, 53, 54, 95
Baumol, W., 3, 4, 5, 99
Bernoulli process, 7, 15, 55
Blocks and treatments, 20, 21, 23, 80-88

Cash flows: independence, 16, 29, 30; normality, 15, 16, 25-30; random versus predictable, 7; stability of means, 16-20; stability of variances, 16-20, 30-32; systematic effects, 18, 20, 21, 23
Compensating balance requirement, 4, 5, 38, 53, 54, 73, 89, 93-96; absolute minimum, 7, 11, 13, 33-59; minimum average, 7, 13, 53, 54, 61-78

Day-of-the-week effects, 20, 21, 23, 80-88
Dynamic programming, 61

Eppen, G., and E. Fama, 37n, 99

Feller, W., 99
Financial officer, role of, 5, 11, 13, 73
Firm A, xv, 5, 11-32, 33, 35, 38-46, 48, 49, 54, 61, 67-73, 80-94
Forecasting, 13, 80, 89-92, 95; day-of-the-week effects, 20, 21, 23, 80-88; harmful aspects, 89-92; systematic effects, 18, 20, 38, 80-88; third-of-the-month effects, 20, 21, 23, 80-88
Freeman, H., 99
Frost, P., 38n, 53, 73, 99

Gaussian (Normal) function, 4, 15, 34, 64-67, 73, 75-78
Gibson, W., 99
Girgis, N., 99

Hausman, W., xv, 44n, 99

Idle cash balances, 4, 35
Independence of cash flows, 16, 29, 30
Invisible costs, 11

Janssen, C., 62n, 99

Keynes, J., 3, 99
Kolmogorov-Smirnov test, 15, 16, 25-29

Linear adjustment model, 89-92

"Matched loading" model, 45-49, 70-73, 83, 87, 88
Maturity of securities, adjustment of, 80-88
Merton, R., xv, 61n
Miller, M., and D. Orr, xv, 3-5, 15, 33, 37, 93-96, 99, 100
Miller-Orr basic two asset model, 7-10, 33-35, 55-59, 93-96; cash flow variance, 7; Gaussian function assumption, 7; independence of daily cash flows, 7, 34 (*see also* Statistical tests); robustness of model, 8; rules for cash-security conversion, 7, 34; stability of cash flow distribution, 16 (*see also* Statistical tests); stochastic cash flows, 7, 34 (*see also* Statistical tests); two parameter control limit, 7, 34. *See also* compensating balance requirement.
Miller-Orr, extensions of, 33-88, 93-96
— absolute minimum compensating balance models, 33-59, 79-88; four and five asset model, 33, 50-53; "matched loading" model, 45-49, 83, 88; three asset Orr model, 33, 36; two asset asymmetric transaction cost model, 43-45, 55, 82, 88
— minimum average compensating balance models, 61-88; adjusted asymmetric transaction cost model, 70-73, 86, 88; adjusted "matched loading" model,

103

Miller-Orr, extensions of (cont.)
70-73, 87, 88; adjusted symmetric transaction cost model, 69, 70, 73, 85, 88; "relaxed" model with penalties, 61-69, 73, 75-78, 84, 88
— need for, 37, 38, 53, 54
— three asset simulation model, 11, 38-43, 79-88
Mills, H., 90, 90n, 100

Neave, E., 100
"Newsboy problem," 66, 67, 77, 78
Normality of cash flows, 15, 16, 25-29

Opportunity cost, 3, 5, 8, 33, 34, 55, 56, 61-66
Orgler, Y., 100
Orr, D., 8, 15, 33, 36, 37, 54, 63n, 89, 90n, 100. *See also* Miller, M., and D. Orr
Outliers, 16, 20, 23, 26-29, 32

Paretian flows, 8, 15, 16
Penalty costs, 62-78
Poisson distribution, 16
Policy constraints of firms, 4, 5, 13
Porteus, E., 100

"Relaxed" minimum average compensating balance model, 62-78, 84-88

"Rigid" minimum average compensating balance model, 61
Runs test of cash flows, 16, 29, 30

Scholes, M., xv
"Sharp pencil" approach, 5, 89, 90
Siegel, S., 100
Simulation of the models, 38-43, 79-88
Statistical tests: blocks and treatments, 20, 21, 23; independence of cash flows, 16, 29, 30; normality of cash flows, 15, 16, 25-30; runs test of independence, 16, 29, 30; stability of cash flow means, 16-20; stability of cash flow variances, 16-20, 30-32

Third-of-the-month effects, 20, 21, 23, 80-88
Transaction costs, 3, 8, 33, 34, 35, 55; asymmetric, 43-49, 55; estimation by simulation, 40-42; "lumpy," 8, 44, 55; proportional, 8, 44; symmetric, 8, 33. *See also* Miller-Orr, extensions of
Transactions demand for money, 3
Treatments and blocks, 20, 21, 23, 80-88

Weitzman, M., 44n, 100

Urban, G., xv

About the Authors

Richard B. Homonoff is President of Boston Economic Associates, Inc., a Cambridge, Massachusetts consulting firm; he has also been an economist for a major consulting firm working with government and industry. Mr. Homonoff received the S.B. in physics and electrical engineering from the Massachusetts Institute of Technology, pursued graduate study in operations research at Stanford University, and received the S.M. in finance from the Sloan School of Management at the Massachusetts Institute of Technology.

David Wiley Mullins, Jr., received the B.S. in administrative sciences from Yale University and the S.M. in finance from the Sloan School of Management at the Massachusetts Institute of Technology. He has taught at M.I.T. and Harvard University and has been a consultant to both industry and non-profit organizations. On completion of the Ph.D. in economics and finance at the Massachusetts Institute of Technology, he will become an assistant professor of business administration at the Harvard University Graduate School of Business. He is also a member of the Board of Directors of Boston Economic Associates, Inc.